Praise for *The Worry-Free Mind*

"In *The Worry-Free Mind*, Carol Kershaw and Bill Wade offer solid clinical experience, case studies, clear explanations, and many simple exercises to show readers how they can live worry-free lives full of possibility. Accept their invitation!"

—Robert B. McNeilly, MBBS, coauthor, *Healing With Words*

"*The Worry-Free Mind* is a delightful book filled with wisdom, insight and tips for dealing with our everyday problems. So many of us deal with worry, stress, and the problems of life that tend to slow us down and put us off-track. If you want to understand yourself better, find more control and satisfaction, this is a *must* read!"

—Jeffrey L. Fannin, PhD, author, *Thought Genius*

THE
WORRY-FREE
MIND

TRAIN YOUR BRAIN,
CALM THE STRESS SPIN CYCLE,
AND DISCOVER A HAPPIER,
MORE PRODUCTIVE YOU

Carol Kershaw, EdD and Will Wade, PhD

CAREER
PRESS
Wayne, NJ

THE WORRY-FREE MIND
EDITED BY STACEY FISCHKELTA
TYPESET BY PERFECTYPE, NASHVILLE, TENNESSEE
Cover design by Brian Moore
Cover photo by nevodka/shutterstock
Printed in the U.S.A.

To order this title, please call toll-free 1-800-CAREER-1 (NJ and Canada: 201-848-0310) to order using VISA or MasterCard, or for further information on books from Career Press.

The Career Press, Inc.
12 Parish Drive
Wayne, NJ 07470
www.careerpress.com

Library of Congress Cataloging-in-Publication Data
CIP Data Available Upon Request.

To our family

ACKNOWLEDGMENTS

We wish to thank Joni Rodgers for helping us get this project off the ground. Our very best to Jill Marsal, our literary agent, who supported this project and found our publisher. Thanks also to Stephanie Land, who provided invaluable editorial assistance.

Our appreciation to Roxanna Erickson-Klein, Jeff Zeig, Michael and Diane Yapko, Steve Lankton, and Alex and Annellen Simpkins for their invaluable support through the years.

Thanks to Ann Byrd for her priceless executive assistant help and to Richard Byrd for his video and artwork for this book.

Thanks to Michael Pye and Lauren Manoy at New Page Books. We appreciate your support throughout this project.

Finally, to our family and friends who always had positive and supportive comments, you have always been there for us.

DISCLAIMER

This book is not designed to replace medical or psychological treatment for a serious health condition. Please seek professional help if you have questions about your physical or psychological health.

CONTENTS

What's That Noise?

Is that bathroom faucet dripping again? Are you sure those documents will get to your client before noon? Does it seem like your mom's health is going downhill lately? Can you afford any of those colleges your daughter is applying to? What's up with that "check engine" light on your dashboard? Why doesn't your spouse understand that—wait. Did you remember to sign those documents before they went to your client?

At 3:30 a.m., the hamster wheel in your head is going 90 mph. At 4:30 a.m., you tell yourself, "I could still get two hours of sleep." At 5:30 a.m., you're still hoping for a catnap. At 6:30 a.m., your alarm clock jolts you awake to face another exhausting day. Multiple stout coffees power you through nine hours at the office. At home, a glass of wine helps you unwind for the evening. After a few hours of fitful sleep, though, your thoughts are spinning, and you're staring at the clock. Again.

What if You Could Flip a Switch and Reverse That Seemingly Unstoppable Cycle?

The day-to-day demands of work and family will always be there; the fear, uncertainty, and stress, however, is a choice you make—or unmake. How would it change your life, health, and relationships if you replaced your fatigue, self-doubt, and constant worry with energy, confidence, and calm? If you've been wondering why the negatives in your life seem to overwhelm the good things, or why your mind won't turn off that incessant worrying, it's time to take control.

With our easy-to-implement tools and exercises, you can:

- Shatter the illusions that keep you in a constant state of worry.
- Meet everyday challenges with clarity and confidence.
- Free your mind for the larger, more joyful task of being fully, gladly alive.

We'll help you think outside the rules and boundaries you've set for yourself—consciously and unconsciously—and upgrade your beliefs and habits to break the cycle of worry that's been wearing you down.

Discover a Calmer, Happier Version of Yourself

How do you go from worry and rumination to a calm and peaceful mind? Tim Ferris, *New York Times* bestselling author of *The 4-Hour Workweek*, said, "You don't have to be Superman to get Superman results; you just need a better toolkit." We've got that toolkit right here, filled with transformative tools and practices that are exploding people's expectations of what is possible. Groundbreaking research in neuroplasticity, epigenetics, and quantum physics has revealed that you don't have to be a victim of genes, circumstances, or your mind. The construction of your physical and emotional reality depends on where you choose to place your attention. If your mind focuses on the negative, your reality will look pretty negative, too, which can cause you to live in a constant state of worry. But now the ability to heal your negative thinking, enjoy the present, manage your mind, and change the harmful habits, perceptions, and behaviors that fuel your worry is at your fingertips.

In *The Worry-Free Mind*, we'll teach you how to quickly calm yourself whenever worry or fear threatens to overwhelm you, and how to set up your environment to support the change you desire. Through easy, approachable applications of the latest neuroscience, we'll enable you to tangibly, quantifiably retool the way your brain works so you can break free from damaging patterns and wake up to a happier, healthier, more vibrant life.

How We Know It Works

Together, we have more than 60 years of experience helping people just like you calm their fears, ease their worry, and take steps to create a better future. *The Worry-Free Mind* is for anyone who finds that incessant worry is ruining his or her quality of life. By identifying the main factor in the brain change process and developing ways to harness the dynamic and healing capabilities of the mind, we've been able to help thousands of patients overcome difficult circumstances and devastating life shocks, as well as cope with the ordinary day-to-day troubles that can wear a person down. We expect you'll be as surprised and delighted as they were to discover that it's possible—and not even that complicated—to rewire your mind and transform your life.

The primary goal of this book is to help you build a resilient inner life that can manage the life shocks—those sudden unpleasant jolts that come out of the blue and knock you off your path toward your goals and slow your progress toward becoming the person you want to be. We take you through eight powerful brain change tools based in research from neuroscience, biofeedback, clinical hypnosis, and the best psychotherapeutic approaches that we have successfully used to get results.

In our work as clinicians we know what works to help not only calm the worrying mind but develop the mental muscle you need to cope with simple and extraordinary life challenges. We will show you how to move from merely getting over worry to living in states of joy, happiness, deep connection, and emotional growth.

What's Inside This Book?

The Worry-Free Mind is divided into four parts.

PART I: Place Your Worry Mind on Hold offers an overview of why we worry and briefly explains the neuroscience behind how our brain is wired to protect us. When you learn how your brain operates, you'll be able to use its amazing resources to find the calm, creative center inside that promotes your best possible life and steels you against life shocks.

Chapter 1: Why We Worry begins with a crash course in Worry 101 and introduces the brain-science fundamentals you need to know to understand how and why the tools we give you throughout this book will help you develop and maintain a worry-free state of mind. It also shows you how to interrupt your most worrying mental movies by changing how you pay attention and what you pay attention to.

Chapter 2: Calm Your Fears to Work Through Tough Times explains how to manage the different brain wave frequencies that cause our various mental states—including the ones that make us worry.

Chapter 3: Zone Out to Make Big Decisions explains how you can work to solve problems by encouraging your unconscious mind to provide you with multiple solutions.

Part II: The Brain's Super Powers builds on the strategies that interrupt worry and moves toward teaching you how to change the pattern of your brain's activity through a process by which mental states link to certain thoughts and feelings. Just as a song combines certain patterns of musical notes, thoughts and emotions are created by a certain pattern of neuronal activity. Just as if you change the patterns of notes, you'll have a different song, if you change your mental associations, you will behave differently and recondition the beliefs you hold about yourself that cause you to worry. When you worry your brain fires in a certain sequence;

when you change the firing pattern significantly enough, it makes it more difficult to fall back into worry because the brain perceives a different and more successful reality.

Chapter 4: Deep State Dive to Dissolve Worry and Rumination discusses a powerful way to create new associations to old habitual patterns through the process called neuro-association. Instead of changing your thoughts—an arduous process—or endlessly processing your feelings, you will learn to associate a problem to a specific challenge, a perceptual shift that will open new possibilities. By teaching you to take yourself to the edge of sleep, this brain-change tool will help you automatically access new, healthier thoughts that can have an amazing transformative effect.

Chapter 5: Future Think to Regain Your Optimism continues to build your brain's worry-diminishing neuro-associations "muscle," introducing positive future-thinking and explaining how to align the three pillars in your architecture of beliefs to create the future you desire.

Part III: Train Your State is all about training yourself to access the emotional states you want to experience more often. With intentional and easy practice you'll learn to replace fear with curiosity and develop a nonreactive mind. This neuro-repatterning practice will free you from the emotional baggage of your past and lead you to live a new life in the present.

Chapter 6: Change Your Emotional Channels identifies seven emotional circuits that you can learn to turn on and off at will so you can overcome old emotional conditioning. Through simply practicing the emotional states you desire, you can recondition the mind to avoid allowing your negative emotions to determine your behavior.

Chapter 7: Neuro-Wellness Rituals to Break Through Crises explores the existential crises most of us experience at some point in our lives that may often stimulate the apex of worry. These practices help you quiet the chaotic worry-chatter so you can connect to your desires and dreams and take steps toward making them come true.

Part IV: Ignite Your Life helps you move far beyond the worry mind and gives you the steps to build the Whole Brain State: a mind that is positive, clear, non-reactive, and frequently in flow.

Chapter 8: Banish Worry for Good With That Whole Brain State takes you beyond interrupting and repatterning worry so you can inoculate yourself from worry in the first place. This balanced state, achieved by focusing on the space around the physical objects near you—literally what's *not* there—eliminates any story the mind might create that leads to worry.

Chapter 9: Flow Into SuperMind takes you past the inoculation process into your SuperMind of Flow States, giving you step-by-step directions for using the advanced tools we teach in our workshops. You'll take your mind to the next level where worry has subsided and life is more joyful and optimistic.

In *The Worry-Free Mind,* we not only give you easy and practical tools that really work, we share stories of real people we've treated who overcame their worries to live the life they desired. The stories have more than one purpose. At one level they are reminders that our problems and worries are rarely unique, and reassurance that they can be resolved. At a deeper level, the stories can tap into your own creative unconscious source of solutions and wisdom. They may lead you to recognize positive aspects in yourself, help you identify your untapped potential, build your self-assurance, and stimulate your imagination to take action in your life. We have seen many people make extraordinary changes in their lives by using the strategies and brain-change tools in this book. Our hope is that you will try them, too. We are sure you will find that you are stronger than you realize, that you have greater abilities than you thought, and that your mind is far more powerful than you know. Don't worry, we'll show you how.

PART I

Place Your Worry Mind on Hold

CHAPTER 1

Why We Worry

That the birds of worry and care fly over your
head, this you cannot change, but that they build
nests in your hair, this you can prevent.
—Chinese Proverb

Marie wakes up in the middle of the night, heart pounding. *Is
someone trying to open the kitchen door?* No. It's the plumb-
ing. Her husband snores softly beside her, but she feels utterly
alone in the dark as her mind starts racing. Instead of drifting
back to sleep, watching pleasant dreams unwind, she'll now lie
awake for hours, viewing an endless slide show of the big and little things she worries about all day: two kids struggling through
adolescence; the possibility that her husband might lose his job,
leaving her as the sole wage earner; her aging parents requiring

more care than their fixed income provides; and the house—it's turned into a money pit they'll never climb out of.

By the time we met Marie, the strain of her incessant anxiety and sleepless nights had begun to take their toll. She was perpetually exhausted, her husband complained she was snippy, she had no patience with her children, and life was starting to look joyless and gray. And when she tried to imagine the future, all she could envision was more of the same. When we asked Marie what she thought might be the first step toward feeling better, she said, "Sleep. Sleep used to give me a break from that B-movie in my head, but now...." She shrugged wearily, her eyes bloodshot and pleading. "How do I turn it off? How do I stop worrying about all these things I have to do and be and—worse yet—all these pointless things that are either out of my control or haven't even happened yet?"

We asked her what she wanted. "I want to control my mind," she said. "I want to be more relaxed and confident. I want to believe things will work out so I don't feel we're on the edge of crisis all the time." She added reluctantly, as if it might be too much to hope for, "I would love to do some things for myself, like walk by the ocean and watch the seagulls soar over the water."

Disbelief washed over her face when we told her we could help. She was about to discover how to use her brain to create the life she yearned for.

You can, too.

You picked up this book. You read the first page. That tells us you want to change. You want to free yourself from worry. You want to end the spin cycle that keeps you awake at night. You want to open your eyes in the morning with a surge of hope and joy. You want to blaze through a productive day uninterrupted by a mental horror show of dour possibilities and impending obstacles.

You've already taken the first step. We're here to help you with the rest of the journey.

Believe in Your Abilities

You didn't always worry, right? In fact, you most likely came into the world with a sense of fearlessness and expectation. If life went well, you had no lack of self-confidence and were enormously curious about life and how it worked. Consider when you began to walk: You mastered a complicated motor activity that took patience, resilience, and the willingness to literally and figuratively stand on your own two feet. You had to master balance, shift your weight, move forward without falling, and notice potential obstacles in the way, all at the same time.

Simultaneously, you learned a variety of emotional tasks. By learning to walk, you had to learn courage, the guts to try something you had never done before. You learned persistence, getting up every time you fell down, pushing through the pain. You learned how to take a risk, knowing you might fall but trying again anyway. You learned how to face your fears and walk through them. And you learned how to make a commitment to a goal.

You unconsciously recorded all of these accomplishments so you could draw from them for the rest of your life. They are there within you right now, ready to give you all the strength and support you need.

So then why are you worried all the time?

The Consequence of Mistaking a Lion for a Rock

The answer has to do with the fact that our world has evolved faster than we have. Early humans developed the ability to quickly perceive and respond to threats. Physical survival was uncertain, and when in doubt assuming danger increased their odds for survival. If they saw a rock and mistook it for a lion, adrenaline shot through their bodies and prepared them for potential danger. If they saw a lion and mistook it for a rock, they were lunch. Erring on the side of caution was the safe alternative, and not harmful because our ancient ancestors performed more physical labor than we do and worked the stress chemicals out of the body.

Fast-forward 15,000 years.

In our world, physical threats are less likely, while emotional pressures are more complex. But we still have that baseline "fight or flight" instinct, just like our ancestors. This "dog-eat-dog" world we live and work in stimulates our primitive fears and survival skills. But living at a perpetual code-orange level of threat and hyper-alertness often causes a cascade of over-arousal, triggering fear chemicals that age the body and keep the mind in a constant state of tension and worry. This intense stress response may contribute to heart attacks, lowered immune response, cancer, and conflict in social relationships.

What you think, feel, and believe impacts the genetic expression in your body on a daily basis. You are your own genetic engineer. You can influence your health and longevity, or your illness and degeneration. Without learning to regulate your internal environment, you can trigger toxic chemical processes in the body that can have devastating effects.[1] DNA is not destiny, but negative thoughts can actually turn on any one of 1,200 stress genes, many of which can lead to chronic illness, depression, and despair.

Your brain can highjack your emotions in a second. Perhaps your early life experiences taught you that it was safer to live in a hyper-alert state and by now, it only takes a little setback or unpleasant surprise to find yourself right back in the middle of anxiety and worry. When this happens often enough, deep within you the cycle you've lived with for so long begins to spiral out of control: You worry about a perceived threat, fear causes you to overreact, making the situation worse, which makes you worry more, which makes you overreact, which makes the situation worse.

And the whole time, that lion you were so worried about was probably just another rock.

We Worry Because of the Brain's Negative Bias

Now you understand why your brain is designed to worry first and think through situations second. We tend to scan the environment for danger, even when we meet friendly people or are in a safe situation. Our brains have the tendency to perceive threat and react to negative input more strongly than positive input. In fact, it's easier to give more attention to negative feelings than positive ones because we tend to overexamine the FUD factor: fear, uncertainty, and doubt. This is called the brain's *negative bias*.

Your brain reacts so quickly it will tell you if a person is trustworthy in a fraction of a second, even if you don't consciously see the person's face. In a study to test this ability, real and computer-generated faces were flashed at a speed below conscious perception. The results showed that the brain recognizes whether a person looks trustworthy.[2] We quickly form negative judgments of others when we decide they don't—even though there is no confirming data. This perceptual capacity connects to our ability to manage fear and anxiety. When you recognize someone is trustworthy, you feel calm. When you perceive someone is untrustworthy, you feel threatened and anxious.

Worry is the tendency to dwell in anxiety and uncertainty over real or imagined problems, cutting straight to the negative judgment, often without pausing for a reality check. The resulting agitation will cause you to incessantly problem-solve and search for different outcomes without ever finding relief. If you are a worrier, you may find yourself attempting to explore all the possible things that can go wrong so you can be prepared. Think about the dour old saws that push you in that direction:

Forewarned is forearmed.

If you want something done right, do it yourself.

Trust no one.

The problem with this approach to life is that you will never feel completely ready for those imaginary bad outcomes. So you keep worrying. "What if...?" is a common question worriers ask themselves, and they fill in the blanks with the worst possible future.

Rumination is a more intense form of worry: an obsessive and repetitive review of distressing factors without the ability to focus on solutions. You might tell yourself that developing contingency plans for possible disasters makes you feel more in control of your life, but chronic rumination—constantly running your own personal Stephen King horror movie marathon in your head—can lead to physical problems such as headaches, gastrointestinal issues, insomnia, and generalized body pain.

How Worrywarts Are Born

Identifying danger is helpful in a crisis where there's an actual threat, but when you develop a worry pattern based on habitual states of overarousal, your sympathetic nervous system turns on high, increasing heart rate, body inflammation and muscle tension, elevated blood pressure, and creating an internal jittery sensation.

Under prolonged negative stress, the brain loses access to its resting states, so it's difficult to fully relax, to sleep deeply, and nearly impossible to come back to a calm emotional center. Your body tenses, your mind ruminates, and you generally feel out of sorts. In this state the brain forms new neural pathways, creating roadmaps for future perspectives, emotions, thoughts, perceptions, and behaviors—and all of them will be colored by the current mental state in which the maps were drawn. Your brain starts weaving large and small life shocks into a pattern of limiting beliefs and rules for living that create anxious, fearful, and moody thinking, and interfere with clarity, follow-through, confidence, and a sense of satisfaction. You develop a habit of defending yourself, which results in poor relationships, compromised health, business failure, and emotional paralysis.

You are now executive producer of a horror movie you can watch any time in the privacy of your own mental theater. Just add popcorn. The movie gravitates from one issue after another, escalating in intensity as it shows you how your problems will continue to plague you and keep you from success in all areas of life, how you can't have what you want, how people are against you and always will be, how you may be sued because of it, how all of your material things will be taken from you, you will end up on the street as a homeless person, and have interminable insomnia for the rest of your life, and no more birthday parties.

Breathe.

Try It Now

Here's a quick and easy mental exercise: Review one of your personal horror flicks for a moment. Are you in the audience observing what happens, or are you an actor in the movie, directly experiencing the event? If you are the observer—good news! You can change the movie easily. If you are the actor, you can change your lines.

Now try this:

- Imagine you're flying up in a helicopter or hot air balloon to film the event from the top down. Visualize zooming out as the event gets smaller and the world around it comes into view. What do you see? Hey, there's a bird! That cloud looks like a pig. Can you see your house?
- Put yourself in a mental movie theater—one of those big chains—watching that zooming effect on a screen. Now move to the very back row of the theater and watch the scene again from this new perspective. How does the movie look now? Smaller? Less intense? From up high in your hot air balloon, doesn't the world look peaceful? If you're in the back row of the theater, doesn't your film look small? Can you see all the seats where other people might sit? From this perspective, is it possible that your problems aren't unique or as big as they feel, and maybe more manageable than you realize?

If you are the actor, you can change your lines to ones that open into possibility. For example, is it really true you'll have no more birthday parties?

It's easy to let life activate your worst negative thinking and sweep you up in a review of all the negative things that have ever happened to you. But by learning how to coach your brain to have more flexibility and stability, you can create a more positive mindset.

Empowered Perspectives

New behaviors automatically emerge when you deliberately shift into a new mental state, such as calm, so our first goal will be to help you retrain your nervous system so that it exists in a less-fear-driven state. Then you can retrain the contents of your mind. As you learn to regulate your body's response to surprises and interrupt your mind's natural tendency to worry or ruminate, you'll develop the ability to stay in happier mental states for longer periods of time.

Many of our clients have been dubious at first. "It can't be that easy. Don't I need to talk about how badly my parents treated me?"

It's certainly helpful to understand your relationship with your parents and figure out how you adopted certain thinking patterns. Certainly, all of your early experiences have had an impact on your daily perception of the world. But endlessly reviewing the past and regurgitating every injustice or dissatisfaction won't move you forward. It doesn't help you find solutions and experience more joy in life. Shake up your thinking patterns, however, and you can break free of your past and forge a vibrant future.

Author Anne Lamott said, "My mind is a bad neighborhood I try not to go into alone."[3] This strategy may work for a while, but if you really want to make a change, you need to get in there and get to work.

The Science Behind Happily Ever After

Marie, the worried insomniac you met at the beginning of this chapter, did eventually get some sleep, regained her equilibrium, and went on to lead her life with confidence and optimism. How? By learning to calm her mind through powerful interventions we've developed based on three neuroscience discoveries:

1. **With practice, you can rewire your brain.** It's a process called self-directed neuroplasticity. Your emotions, patterns of behavior, attitudes, and perspectives are all connected to your mental states. How and where you focus your attention determine the mental state where you spend the most time. Change the focus of your attention and you can change the mental state you live in.

2. **By self-regulating and managing your beliefs, feelings, and behaviors, you can make changes and live in happier mental states for longer periods of time.** Living in a state of worry, always running the worst possible future movies in your head, keeps your mental

state in constant crisis mode. But when you learn to master yourself through awareness and self-regulation, you begin to see the world more clearly and react to your experiences appropriately. For example, if you find yourself irrationally lashing out at people, through self-regulation you may recognize that what you really need is to let off some steam, so you start taking the stairs instead of the elevator every day. In this way, you're consciously choosing a strategy to achieve the mental state you desire instead of spinning blindly in a mental state that does neither you nor anyone else any good.

3. **Your body reflects your mind.** You know all too well that worry can give you an upset stomach or headache. Your mental state impacts your physical state on a moment-to-moment basis, sending out unconscious thoughts and feelings that direct your behavior. When you consciously direct calming thoughts to your mind, however, you can effect astounding changes in your nervous system. You can actually rewire your brain to change your mind, and reprogram your mind to change your body.

In our research and clinical experience, we've learned that your brain functions optimally when you train and condition the mind and nervous system to be calm. When you also set up your environment to support and sustain that state of calm, such as taking a break from watching the evening news or going on a social media hiatus for a while, you can diminish the anxiety and rumination in your day-to-day life.

But what happens when unforeseen events—drama or even tragedy that inevitably comes in some form to almost all of us—rocks our world?

Life Shocks

You're going along when suddenly, something unexpected throws you off course, something shocking, stunning, and, for a while, immobilizing. We call this sudden stress event a *life shock*. It comes out of nowhere. It hurts. It stops you in your tracks. A storm, financial setback, emotional abuse, loss of a job, illness, some heartbreaking disappointment at work or with your partner—an experience like this often affects your sense of safety, connection to others, or feelings of worth. Life shocks can happen at any age, but when we're young they're more difficult to manage. They can shut down our courage to take risks and block our initiative to discover the purpose and gifts we could have—and should have—offered to the world.

When we've been hurt, when we're under stress, fighting to regain our equilibrium, our behaviors change. Our primal survival instincts emerge, determined to protect us, sometimes in destructive ways. For example, if you feel fragile, easily hurt, or even outraged, you might automatically protectively pull inward. In your isolation, you might start worrying that your friends and family are against you, which can soon lead you to start living on high alert, which then leads you to react poorly to ordinary situations without understanding why. For many, even as the shock fades, a legacy of worry lingers just below the surface.

The more you worry that this same life shock will occur again, even unconsciously, the more fearful and anxious you feel. You wake up in the morning feeling uneasy, almost a trembling in your stomach. *What's causing this bad feeling?* you ask yourself. Your mind's attention goes from one worry to another nonstop—a difficult conversation you need to have with your spouse, an employee you have to lay off, financial worries, your aging parents—and cycles around to start all over, always focused on the worst possible outcomes. You feel alone, trying to solve problems without knowing what the problem actually is.

Everyone experiences life shocks. Not everyone lets them take control of their lives. To break the cycle of worry, you're going to have to make some changes.

Attention and Self-Regulation

Part of your problem is that you're paying attention to all the wrong things. Mihaly Csikszentmihalyi, author of *Flow*, noticed, "What we pay attention to, and how we pay attention, determines the content and quality of life."4 So if your attention is entirely focused on what could go wrong, life is going to feel very unstable indeed. But if you can change the focus of your attention, you can change your brain and your internal experience of life.

In the 1970s, biofeedback researchers discovered that people could become aware of very subtle internal sensations, such as heart rate, hand temperature, and muscle tension. Each sensation is connected to a particular state of consciousness. Once you become aware of those sensations—usually possible only with the help of a biofeedback system—you can learn to control them, and thus your state of consciousness.

But we don't need a biofeedback system to make those changes. Later research found that humans can, with practice, raise or lower amplitudes of their own brain waves. Our brain waves are what generate our emotions, so if you can control them, you can more easily recover from painful events and spend more of your life feeling happy (we'll explain how in Chapter 2). You're less likely to step in your own personal ant bed of negative thoughts, emotions and behaviors that make you feel terrible. With practice, you master self-regulation, proving the old adage: "Energy flows where attention goes."

Arousal Levels (Not as Much Fun as They Sound)

Our brain acts a bit like our own personal branch of Homeland Security, assessing threats and setting our minds to the corresponding arousal levels it thinks will be best suited to keep us safe. When life goes well, your brain is in an optimal arousal state: not too tense and not too relaxed. You're chilling in that Goldilocks middle ground, where your mental and physical state is *just right*. Obviously, dangerous events—like three bears walking in the door—require a high level of arousal for you to react quickly, but normally as you learn to successfully respond to surprising but non-life threatening situations with low to medium arousal, you can negotiate the bumpy road and quickly return to a calm mind.

Worry, however, keeps you stuck in a state of high arousal, and when you become over-aroused in a situation that isn't dangerous, your responses will be out of whack, reacting to threats that don't exist. Meanwhile, if you are depressed, you'll be under-aroused in situations that need a heightened response, which can be equally debilitating. Being over-aroused and frazzled, or being under-aroused or disengaged, ruins our efforts to be at our best in all situations.

Our goal is to help you learn to self-regulate so that your arousal levels leave you relaxed but alert, so you don't respond with worry to stressful events and can perform optimally the rest of the time. We want you to become more aware of how you generally respond to situations: This is your default state, your resting mental space.

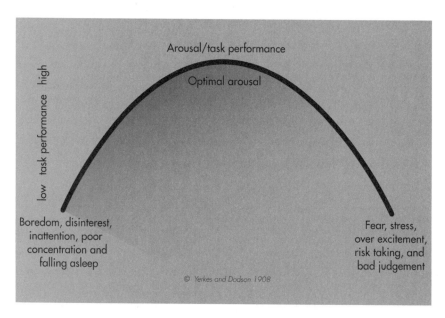

Emotional Adventures of a Go-Go Girl

Rachel, a high-powered telecom industry executive, was responsible for making financial decisions at her company. All day she ruminated over whether she was making the right choices. She got so scared of making the wrong call that eventually she started to freeze up every time she had to make a decision. The fear of making a mistake was overwhelming and making it hard for her to do her job well. Her boss had started hinting that he wasn't happy with her performance, and the stress was keeping her awake at night, and making her tired and grumpy around her friends.

We asked her, "How do you want to feel?"

"I want to stop worrying all the time," she said. "I want to make decisions quickly and feel confident about them."

We suggested that Rachel try to remember a time when she felt calm and confident.

"Easy," she said. "I spent some time learning psychological strategies in corporate training, and they taught me how to calmly diffuse potential conflict at work. It was totally fascinating. Right up my alley."

Her demeanor shifted before our eyes, from worried and weary to calm and curious.

"Great," we told her. "Remember that feeling. We're going to work on getting you to feel that way more often. Every time you feel worried or scared, you're going to be able to snap yourself out of it, and eventually this calm state is going to be where you spend most of your time."

Because the mind's tendency is to wander from one worry to another and then to disconnected subjects, maintaining one mental state for a period of time is a skill that requires practice. It's more difficult than it seems.

The next time you're feeling worried, try focusing on your breath for one minute. Notice what happens? You'll find it is impossible to worry and focus on the breath at the same time.

Now think about a problem. Problems are all about how you define them, and sustained in patterns of thinking or how you pay attention. If your definition leaves no possibility that the problem isn't as hard to solve as it seems, you've painted yourself into a corner, and there's nothing to do but sit there and worry. But there are always many solutions to a problem, even though some require thinking outside the mental box you construct.

Milton Erickson, the famous psychiatrist who was chosen as one of the top 25 clinicians in the United States by *Life* magazine, used to say, "Whatever you can imagine, you can accomplish."

Erickson, who lived in Phoenix, used to ask his students to think about this problem: *How many ways can you travel from Phoenix to Tucson?* His students came up with the usual answers:

car, plane, bus, train. Erickson challenged them to relax and allow their unconscious minds to suggest other ideas. In just a few moments, the creative ideas were zinging around the room: take a hot air balloon, fly a plane around the world backward, tunnel under the ground.

"Very good," said Erickson in his mischievous way, "but your unconscious mind has many other solutions. Try again."

Now the class moved further outside the box: teleportation, astral projection, ostrich racing. It was an exercise in learning that the frame you place on a problem limits its solutions, and if you let your mind soar, astounding ideas emerge and you open up futures that were never before accessible to you. We used this technique to help Rachel open up to the possibilities in front of her and achieve greater confidence in her ability to problem-solve and make decisions.[5]

How Your Personal Stories Contribute to Worry and Anxiety

The stories you tell yourself change how you behave.

The unique narratives we construct about ourselves lock in our story about what we believe is possible. But we can unlock those possibilities by changing our story. We can't undo the pain we've experienced—and we all experience it—but we can learn to manage it by reshaping the stories we tell ourselves about those painful events. Joan Didion said, "We tell ourselves stories in order to live,"[6] but the story itself can help or hinder *how* you live. Change the story and you can change your perspective, and then all things are possible.

Stories Are Mental Fuel

Amber, a CPA at a large tax law firm, became involved in a conflict with a coworker and began to worry about her spreading negative rumors. Her coworker, Reba, was climbing the ladder to management and was on the fast track to be promoted. Reba had a reputation for talking negatively about everyone except those in power, to whom she kowtowed. Amber tried to have conversations with her to work out a difference of opinion in how to accomplish the office goals, but Reba would avoid the encounters and could be seen having covert talks with others. Amber felt disempowered as time went on and didn't know what to do.

We asked Amber what story she was telling herself. She described a scenario in which everyone turned away from her and her boss was unhappy with her work. Her next horror scene was of her company laying her off, forcing her to work for much less money somewhere else.

We suggested she change her story so that it was about Reba. As she settled her mind, a new idea popped in. She suggested that perhaps the reason Reba dedicated herself to her work and aimed to receive the most kudos by blocking others' success and spreading negative ideas about them was because she was insecure and lonely. This different story thawed Amber's frozen narrative that told her she could do nothing but suffer and feel constant fear. Her new story allowed Amber to feel empathy for Reba, even as she realized that she could strategically protect herself by staying warm yet aloof.

The more you are wedded to your personal story, the less flexibility you have in choosing a different perspective.

Try It Now

Take a moment for this brief written exercise. Research has shown that writing down negative feelings serves to reinforce them, unless you take the paper they're written on and throw them in the trash.[7] On the flip side, you can calm yourself through simple exercises like writing yourself a kind note. You'll be amazed at the difference it makes when you contemplate your words on paper, so treat yourself to a nice, smooth ink pen, fresh notebook, and a clean sheet of lined paper.

Draw a line straight down the middle to divide the page in half. On the left side, describe your current/default state of mind, the way you feel now on an average day.

- How happy are you on a scale of one to 10, one being despondent and 10 being blissful?
- Does the way you feel, mentally and physically, change the way you participate in your life, work, and relationships?
- How do you feel about how you feel? Is this the way you want to live?

On the right side of the paper, describe the state of mind in which you'd like to be living. Write the story of what you want in your life. Is it more adventure, more security, more peacefulness, more community, or a better relationship?

- What would have to happen over the next year in order to have more of what you want?
- How would a calmer mind change the way you enjoy and participate in your life, work, and relationships?
- When you reality-check the worries that keep you up at night, can you see yourself being happy, even if these issues don't resolve the way you want them to—or resolve at all? If not, keep trying until you are able to imagine a future where everything has worked out. It doesn't matter if you believe it will happen—you just need to be able to picture it. The more frequently you do this, the more you'll start to believe it's possible.

Be your own personal detective; don't accept the easy answers. Self-awareness is the first step to finding peace and learning to operate from a calm mental state. Repeat this self-assessment after one week, after 30 days, and after 90 days of practicing the tools and techniques in this book. Your progress will encourage you as you continue toward your goal of a calm, worry-free mind.

Go Deeper: Assess Your Emotional Reactivity and Self-Regulation

Let's crack out another clean sheet of paper and divide it right down the middle again.

You'll answer the following 20 questions under each heading, rating your response on a scale of one to 10:

1 = very little/seldom

5 = somewhat/sometimes

10 = extremely/always

Once again, the left side will be that default state where you are now, and the right side will be where you want to be.

Emotional Reactivity

1. How reactive do you get when people disappoint you?
2. Do you tend to become anxious around people?
3. Do you tend to avoid people?
4. How cheery are you?
5. When you are under stress, do you tend to become anxious, depressed, or a mixture?
6. How often are you upset with others?
7. How fulfilled are you now?
8. How judgmental are you toward others?
9. How long can you hold a positive state of mind?
10. How much do you find yourself blaming others for your feelings?

Self-Regulation

1. How able are you to bring your mind back to a pleasant place after an upset?
2. How easily can you make changes in your behavior?
3. How would you rate your willpower?
4. How alive do you feel?
5. How often do you numb yourself?

6. How often do you use sweets or carbohydrates, such as chocolate chip cookies, for personal therapy?
7. How rigid is your thinking?
8. Do you engage in habitual worry?
9. Do you feel victimized by others?
10. How often do you feel angry?

What you'll see when you compare the two columns is a graphic road map showing specific areas where a gap exists between where you are and where you want to be. These are the areas where you'll want to focus your attentions and your intentions as we go forward together.

You've learned about the natural tendency of the brain to focus on negative events and scan the environment for threat. Worry and rumination, those personal Stephen King horror mind-movies about the terrible outcomes that possibly await, keep your anxiety high rather than allowing you to calm down enough to find a solution to your problems or put them in perspective. These movies will become part of your life story unless you commit to training yourself to reside in a calmer mental state. You've learned that worry and rumination are the result of states of over-arousal, and that every mental state is caused by patterns of emotion, beliefs, and behaviors. When you shift your mental state, you shift those emotions, beliefs, and behaviors, and ultimately you change your reality.

Power Thought: *With brain training, you can shift your mental state to access more positive patterns of behaviors, perspectives, emotions, and attitudes.*

Now that you have a good idea of how the mind works, you are ready to discover how the brain actually puts us in certain frames of mind. Then you'll be ready to experience your first powerful brain-change tool to completely shut off anxiety and worry.

CHAPTER 2

Calm Your Fears to Work Through Tough Times

Every state of consciousness we experience
is a combination of one or more of the
four categories of brain waves.
—Anna Wise, *Awakening the Mind*

Apollo 13 gained fame as the problem-plagued 1970 mission to the moon, memorialized by the movie of the same name. But it turns out the mission was bedeviled even before an explosion forced its astronauts to abort and jerry-rig their way back to Earth. During their training, the astronauts became repeatedly nauseous and several suffered seizures. The project directors thought escaping rocket fuel fumes might be the culprits, so they called up research psychologist Barry Sterman at UCLA to see whether he could determine if this was the problem. Sterman had been studying sleep patterns in cats, and had determined that when they were relaxed, the animals generated the 14 Hertz brain wave frequency called sensorimotor rhythm (SMR). Curious as to whether the cats could produce this frequency at will, he hooked them up to an EEG machine, which allowed him to read their brain waves. Whenever they elevated their sensorimotor rhythm, he rewarded them with milk and chicken broth. The cats were quick studies and soon were elevating their SMR rhythm to get milk more frequently.

The NASA request was a completely different project, but Sterman agreed to test the rocket fuel for NASA by exposing a group of his cats to the fumes. Sure enough, many had the same reaction as the astronauts: The rocket fuel was indeed causing the seizures. The researchers learned one more astounding thing: The cats that had been trained to elevate their sensorimotor rhythm reacted very differently than the untrained cats to the toxin. Sterman discovered that the cats that had been conditioned to produce more 14 Hz brain waves were able to overcome the effects of the toxin in their systems. By accident, Sterman had discovered a brain training process, now called neurofeedback, that would eventually have remarkable positive effects on the way we treat anxiety, depression, and a host of other mental health issues. His research brought us amazingly good news. If cats could change their brain activity and improve their well-being, so could humans.

Altering your brain's activity and in turn your corresponding mental states (for example, from sad to happy) also allows you to control your reactions to what happens to you. The trick is to learn to shift your attention away from whatever is causing you stress or anxiety. When you interrupt a worry train of thought, you trigger important physiological changes. Just shifting your attention away from a problem releases nitric oxide, which reduces inflammation and activates a healing process that blocks stress hormones, lowers blood pressure and heart rate, and leads to clarity of mind. It's a conditioning process that takes practice, but once you master it you can calm your mind and body at will, which will make a dramatic change in your outlook on life.

When you focus on something calming rather than your internal ruminations, you can't worry. Several exercises in this book will teach you how to develop this attention shift. Their effectiveness will have a ripple effect. Once you learn to live more frequently in a positive, less-worried mental state, you will be able to dissolve the obstacles that are keeping you from your goals, which should make you feel more in control and able to take greater responsibility for your life, which should in turn set you on a path for success and greater happiness.

Almost any activity that absorbs your attention and puts you in a positive frame of mind will help banish worry. For example, Kelsie, a therapist and one of our students, took a fall that resulted in a severe brain injury. It was debilitating, and afterward she had trouble focusing and thinking clearly. When her doctor told her there was nothing else he could do, she devised her own mental training using repetitive word games and memory practice. Every day she did three crossword puzzles, memorized five new words and their definitions, and also reviewed the words she had learned the previous day. Then she made herself read something boring followed by something interesting, asking herself questions about what she read. In addition, she played Tetris, a game that requires intense concentration. She discovered that her memory especially improved when she made herself replay conversations from the previous day and week. She also learned that she performed better when she was rested. Overall, she found the training invigorating and uplifting, especially as she began to feel that she was making progress. Over about nine months, during which she trained for 20 minutes a day, Kelsie found that with practice her brain circuits could retrain her memory, focus, and stamina, and that the training held over time. She completely recovered her ability to think clearly, and she returned to work.

Word and memory games worked for Kelsie, but you might prefer video games, playing an instrument or singing music, puzzles, athletic play, or exercise. Flow is a state of highly concentrated focus, and while in that state, it becomes impossible to have a worry thought. As with all brain training, the more you do it, the more long-lasting the effects.

The Brain Is a Creature of Habit

Many years ago Donald Goodwin and his colleagues at the Washington Department of Psychiatry conducted a fascinating research study. They had no problem finding volunteers: The experiment required college students to drink to inebriation. Once they were drunk, the students were instructed to memorize nonsense words. They were then tested to see how well they remembered the words they had memorized. After analyzing their scores, the researchers waited for the students to sober up, then tested their memory again. They found the students didn't do as well sober as they did when they were inebriated. To ensure that the difference in scores was not due solely to the passage of time between memorizing the words and the second test, the researchers asked the students to get drunk again. Without allowing the students any time for review, the researchers administered the test again. What they found out was startling. The students did as well on the third test, drunk, as they had on the first test, drunk, and better than they had on the second test when they were sober. The results demonstrated that what you learn in one state of mind, you remember best in that state of mind. So the next time you're frustrated because you've forgotten an important piece of information, try to put yourself back in the state of mind in which you learned the information in the first place. That's how the information was encoded, so that's where it will most likely be retrieved.[1]

The same thing is true for retrieving emotions. We're often taught that in order to solve a problem we should stay with it, worrying it like a dog with a bone, until we find the solution. But that's all wrong. Our brain lays down neural pathways every time we experience something troublesome or worrying. Focusing on the problem or event (such as reliving a past event over and over trying to see what you could have done differently) only keeps those neural patterns active and leaves you stuck in the same mindset you were in when you first encountered the problem. As Einstein himself said, the same level of consciousness that created a problem cannot solve it. However, resources such as confidence, courage, persistence, and optimism are generally encoded when we are in positive mental states. So to gain access, we must return to that positive mental state.

Willing ourselves into a desired mindset takes practice and patience, as our client David discovered. David was trudging through a difficult divorce. He was surprised to find that in addition to the emotions he expected to feel, like anger and sorrow, he was also overwhelmed by worry. Every glimpse into the future gave him heart palpitations. Would the children want to spend holidays with him? Would they turn to some other father figure for support and guidance? What if they never accepted his girlfriend and she found all the drama too much and left him? How was he going to pay for college now that he had lost all his money in the divorce?

David had read many self-help books and followed their advice to the letter, trying to breathe deeply, think pleasant thoughts, and stop worrying. But when he tried to relax and breathe more slowly, he discovered his tension and heart rate increased. The result was a cascade of negative thoughts and feelings, especially at night when he tried to go to sleep. By the time we met with him, he had tried half a dozen techniques, none of which had worked.

We reassured him that he wasn't doing anything wrong; these techniques didn't always work because they didn't take into account how the brain actually operates. The brain is methodical, recording patterns of emotions and behaviors, placing them into memory, and translating them into particular mental states. Unconsciously, we remember which events make us feel a certain way. By calling up our memories of those events, we can trigger the corresponding mental state we were in at the time. But trying to move from a state of intense worry to extreme relaxation in one go is too taxing. You have to build a bridge to get yourself from one extreme state to its opposite. David would need to learn to ease into a new mental state if he wanted to get rid of his worry.

We asked him to imagine that on his way home that night his level of worry was going to be at a 10 on a scale of 1 to 10, with 1 being totally relaxed and 10 at panic (it wasn't a stretch; he was already really close). What activity could he do that would help bring him down to a 9? He said the first thing he would do is turn on some music when he got home. Then we asked him to take the next step and ask himself what would he need to do to move down to an 8? He said he often found it relaxing to take the dog for a walk. We had him plot out every step he could take to get his emotional level down to a 1, and take his mind away from all of the unanswerable questions and fears. These issues don't occur all at the same time, so we would help him figure them out one at a time. Walking with the dog was a superb way of relaxing the mind and connecting with nature. Walking also stimulates the creative mind, so that would be a good time to focus on coming up with a plan to attack one of his fears. We suggested that David visualize himself able to devise creative solutions. It didn't matter if he didn't know specifically what they were because creative solutions often take some time to simmer in the back of the mind. The point was just to imagine having the eureka moment. David experimented with walking and visualization, and soon he reported he felt much better. He believed that he'd find a way to successfully cope should any of the what-ifs he'd once worried about come to pass.

David's worry was fueled by his lack of confidence in his ability to handle all the changes in his life and especially maintain a relationship with his children. To free himself completely, he would need to escape the mindset in which he had learned to worry in the first place. We also reassured him that he would feel better if he stopped trying to predict every issue that could arise as a result of his divorce. In the meantime, however, he needed to find the emotional resources that would eventually allow him to confidently problem solve. With our prodding, he started remembering all the times when he had felt resolved to accomplish something, from getting his master's to learning to play the harmonica. Remembering these moments whenever he started feeling the anxiety creep up on him helped boost his confidence. The more he conditioned his mind with nonreactive states and thoughts, the more creative, resourceful, and resilient he became, until he was able to navigate his post-divorce world with grace and calm.

Experimenting with different relaxation triggers will provide you with a blueprint for altering your emotional make-up. You'll know that if you just need to take the edge off, a quick jog in place will do, and if you need to completely relax, you need to head to the hot tub. And if you're not in a position to do either because you're on an airplane or at work, just remembering how it feels to do that activity will be enough to trigger the corresponding mental state. Accessing the appropriate mental state, whether it is courage, curiosity, or believing that giving up is not an option, is the prerequisite to overcoming any adversity.

Mind Control Is Possible

Our state of mind and emotions are a product of our brain waves. As your neurons fire electrical signals they activate a process in the brain that allows you to accomplish tasks. When everything fires well, you are mentally agile, calmly rocking through the day with ease, comfort, and clear focus. For example, when you are paying bills you must be focused and alert. This requires a fast brain frequency called Beta. When you need to reflect on when you are going to get paid, your brain easily moves into somewhat slower Alpha. If you start to wonder how you will pay for something in the future, your brain will produce even slower Theta to help you come up with a solution. When you then congratulate yourself for resolving your potential problem, your brain will return to Alpha.

A balanced brain—one that easily shifts between brain states with ease and proficiency, sees the world as friendly, safe, and inviting. An unbalanced brain has difficulty shifting brain states, which alters its perceptions of the world. For example, if it gets stuck on a repetitive thought, the stagnation can make you perceive life through a narrow lens colored by threat, danger, and disconnection. If you have trouble shifting from a daydream to paying attention in class, your brain is struggling to move into a new brain state. The good news is that you have more control over your brain states than you think.

The Body/Brain Electric

Your brain is constantly firing electrical impulses that can be measured in hertz, which refers to cycles of electrical activity per second. There are five types of brain waves that range from .05 Hz 100 Hz. The dominant bandwidth determines your brain state, which triggers your emotions. Spend too much or too little time in any of these ranges and you won't function well.

All of these five brain waves are always working at the same time, though their ratios change as your activity changes. However, sometimes one becomes dominant over the other and doesn't retreat even when a new activity calls for a different brain wave. When that happens, trouble ensues. Reading requires a fast frequency to keep you interested in the text; if you get dreamy and bored when you read, it means your slower frequencies are rising instead of your faster ones. If you go to bed but your faster frequencies won't come down so your slow brain waves can come up, you'll be counting sheep for a long time. To know which brain-wave bandwidth you need to aim for when trying to eliminate worry, you need to know more about each.

Our brain uses Beta waves (12 to 35 hertz) for accomplishing cognitive tasks and paying attention. The body is always trying to stay in balance. When you spend too much time in dominant Beta, especially when you need to unwind, you can end up feeling anxious and depressed. For example, let's say company is coming over. You realize you need to clean up, so your Beta kicks in to help you do that. Normally, as you start to clean and see the fruits of your efforts, a new brain wave should take dominance. But if your Beta stays dominant, as you clean you'll start to fret over whether your house is clean enough for company, which will lead you to worry that you don't have enough time to finish, which will make you worry about what your guests will think of you if the house isn't clean. One worry turns into another, and you go around and around until you feel anxious. It can make it difficult to turn off worrisome thoughts and relax. People stuck in Beta tend to hyperfocus, which can then lead to catastrophizing and making problems seem bigger than they really are.

For example, if a mother stuck in Beta hyperfocuses on her son's bad grade, her imagination may go hog wild and convince her that he will never get into the right college.

The mother thinks that by focusing on how to raise her son's grades she is digging for a solution, but repetitively going over a problem without trying to lift yourself into a different mental state leaves you in a box that won't allow a creative solution to emerge. The only way to move out of such rigid thinking is to shift brain states. In this case, the mother would need to expand her frame of reference and connect with different solutions by consciously move from Beta to Alpha.

Alpha ranges from 8 to 12 hertz and provides the comfort we need so we can regenerate our energy after performing a tiring cognitive task that requires Beta, like figuring out our taxes. Alpha is the range of frequencies that can give you the power to ignore discomfort and worrying thoughts, and return to a more comfortable internal place where you can take in information without judgment. An easy way to access Alpha is through meditation or just counting your breaths from 1 to 5 repeatedly for five minutes.

However, you can get stuck in Alpha, which could cause you to be overly chilled out with no sense of urgency about anything. A young person watching television might be hungry, but still not move when his mother tells him it is time for dinner. This is because Alpha has made him so mellow he not only doesn't hear his mother he also doesn't register hunger. Though it is really comfortable, without shifting back into Beta, Alpha doesn't allow you to accomplish much.

Theta provides a slower rhythm at 4 to 7 hertz. Brain waves in this range put you in the mental state right above sleep. They can dissolve worry and rumination, which is why it would be good for the mother we described earlier, worrying herself to pieces over her son's grades, to learn to shift them by deeply relaxing. They also help you heal from illness. Repeated exposure to Theta can reduce emotional eating and enhance feelings of well-being, as well as take you to a highly intuitive state. Unfortunately, too much time in Theta can make you even less connected and less productive than Alpha. Although Theta enables you to pick up intuitive information that could prove to be useful, you must be able to shift into Beta to actually do something with the information.

Delta takes you into the deepest sleep for regeneration and renewal. It reduces cortisol and links to the unconscious mind. During the sleep cycle, Delta releases human growth hormone, dopamine, and serotonin. Delta is important for regenerative sleep.

When awake, people with high amounts of Delta have been found to have increased empathy. In Delta, the electrical activity in your brain is only at about .05 to 3.0 hertz. That's one half to three cycles of energy per second.

If you are chronically in Delta, it could be a sign of brain injury or disease. Though brain-injured people can function somewhat with dominant Delta waves, it slows their capacity to think clearly and they may feel foggy. People caught in Delta tend to have difficulty completing cognitive tasks or suffer major problems with short-term memory. If not treated, chronic Delta that makes the brain sleepier over time is a potential sign of further deterioration of the brain from a degenerative illness. This problem requires intervention by a neurologist.

Finally, there's Gamma. At 35 to 70 hertz, this state encourages a highly focused mind and allows you to increase happiness, have more creative ideas, and formulate plans to accomplish goals. In fact, when you have a sudden intuition, you can thank Gamma. It spiked right before you formed your new idea. Your brain uses this state to block worry and rumination. Increasing Gamma often rids people of their worst worries and enhances feelings of peace and centeredness. However, in order to actively produce it, you must spend quite a while in meditation training. Buddhist monks who are advanced meditators generally show more Gamma activity than novice meditators. Though it might seem ideal to stay in Gamma as much as possible, you must shift back into other brain states to operate in the world. Even Buddhist monks who spend hours meditating must come out of this state to work in the temple.

We tend to learn our dominant mental state through our birth families and life experiences. If you walk around in dominant Beta, you may be hard-driving, task-oriented, and high strung. Those who have a meditation practice often live more in Alpha and are slower to react to people and situations. A Theta-dominant person tends to pick up information about others and may show psychic tendencies. People in whom Delta is dominant may have difficulty getting off the couch and getting things done even as they can also be more thoughtful and deliberate in evaluating data and making decisions. Gamma-dominant people tend to either be Buddhist monks or have logged more than 10,000 hours of meditation, generally focusing on compassion. They tend to have a stable sense of self that creates a sense of inner security no matter the external stressors.

As we get older, each of these five frequencies wax and wane depending on several factors, such as where we focus our attention, our level of physical activity, and our levels of emotional arousal. There are several exercises you can use to deepen or activate your brain waves and eliminate your worried feelings.

Shift Your Attention

How you focus your attention changes your brainwave frequencies, your mental state, and leads to default patterns of thinking that affect how you perceive reality. You view the world through your "default" or favorite mental state. For example, Buddhist monks who meditate on compassion experience the world through the lens of deep abiding connection and compassion. Someone who has been abused is often on hyperalert and in high Beta most of the time; they therefore will have trouble responding to compassion and support, and will tend to hear personal criticism in everyday comments. This state of being hyperalert serves to protect him from being wounded again, but until he learns how to accept help and support, it may be difficult for him to get beyond his pain.

If you can control your attention you can control your feelings, thoughts, and behaviors, which means you also have the ability to increase your own motivation, persistence, courage, curiosity, and even willpower. When you control your attention on purpose, you can accomplish anything humanly possible. As you go through the coming exercises, you will discover you are more powerful than you ever imagined.

Your ability to maintain attention is affected by normal cyclical fluctuations in the neurotransmitters that chemically regulate attention. These fluctuations occur in 90-minute cycles across 24 hours.[2] That means that every 90 to 120 minutes you begin to lose concentration, get sleepy, and need a break. Your slow brain waves increase and efforts to pay attention don't work. In fact, glucose and blood pressure drop every 90 minutes. That's why we usually take our coffee breaks at 10 a.m., 2 p.m., and 4 p.m.— those times dovetail with our biological needs.

But this natural biological cycle works to regenerate energy and attention if we allow it to occur without trying to short-circuit it with stimulants. Our energy is restored once our brain waves are back on track and appropriately balanced in the correct ratios with each other for specific activities. One way to make that happen is to take a little rest until your sleepiness disappears. Don't use caffeinated coffee or worse, the energy drinks that have extremely high levels of caffeine to jolt you into staying with a task longer. You risk sabotaging the immune system that takes care of you, making you vulnerable to illness.

Unfortunately, we can't all just follow our bodies' rhythms and lie down when we get tired. So another way to boost your energy, believe it or not, is to breathe through one nostril at a time. Every 90 to 120 minutes, one of your nostrils has more air coming in and going out. Check it out now. Close your right nostril with your finger, pressing lightly on the outside of the nostril. Notice how much air flows in and out. Then close the left nostril. Which side has more air? If your right side is more open, the left hemisphere is more dominant; and if your left side is more open, the right side is more dominant. When you need new ideas or solutions to problems, lie down on the floor on your right side until the left nostril opens and watch new ideas come flooding in. The result is a balanced brain with equal blood flow to each hemisphere, which makes you feel rested.

Pay Attention to the Big Picture

Rachel was always worried about what people were thinking of her. In work meetings, social gatherings, and even on the phone, she paid close attention to how people responded, the tone of their voices when they spoke to her, and whether they smiled at her. She was convinced people didn't like her much, and she ruminated about it all the time. It was exhausting. The thing is people did like Rachel. But she missed their smiles, their words and sounds of encouragement, their twinkling eyes, and supportive behaviors. Her attention had simply become too narrowly focused on what she perceived to be negative, which had led her to expect only negative interactions.

We always shift our focus from wide to narrow to diffuse and back again. Wide focus gets the bigger picture, like when you drive, and narrow focus picks up details like when you look at one part of a painting. Diffuse attention is more like noticing a mosaic.

Those who worry tend to narrowly focus on a problem, which raises their Beta frequency, which limits their ability to solve the problem and causes them to start ruminating. Narrow focus activates their fight/flight/freeze response and places them into emergency mode. Yet even after a problem has passed, they may still find themselves narrowly focusing on the "what ifs" as a means of protection. The result is that they never move to a state of regeneration, and this intensely focused tension spills over into sleep, recreation, and relationships.

In order to feel more comfortable around others, Rachel needed to learn how to develop flexible attention.

Use Flexible Attention

Having flexible attention means that you can shift from a narrow focus, where all you see is what's in front of you, to a broader one. If you worry and ruminate like Rachel, you may have been unintentionally practicing problem-focused attention for a while instead of giving yourself a break. Only when Rachel finally stopped looking at individual people's expressions for signs of acceptance, and started taking in the generally positive response she got when presenting to or navigating groups, did she learn to let her guard down and stop worrying so much about what kind of impression she was making.

Use Your Peripheral Vision

One common cause for worry and losing flexible attention is major change and uncomfortable situations, the more stressed you feel, the more narrow and inflexible your focus. We met Jodie as she was struggling to adapt to a new job, a new city, and a new relationship. To help her regain her balance and composure, we taught her to use her peripheral vision. It works like this:

Look straight ahead while noticing what is on either side of you. Now focus just straight ahead and let your attention become absorbed in one spot on the wall for a few seconds. Shift your attention and while looking straight ahead begin to notice your peripheral attention. While you are noticing the periphery try to have a worry thought. It is likely difficult. Why? You have just turned on a calmer state.

Mastering the flexibility to move your focus back and forth from narrow to wide is a skill you need every day. We have demands that need both the ability to focus on things that are going well, those that aren't, and then to shift to the bigger picture to keep things in perspective. It's like driving. People with a fear of driving on the highway get stuck because they're focusing too much on how close they are to the side of the road or how close other cars are to them. They miss what's straight ahead, what's behind them, as well as any interesting sights. Overfocusing on everything close up makes our immediate surroundings look scary.

But you can achieve instant calm no matter where or what you are doing when you can shift from a narrow focus to a diffuse one—when you can see the big picture—merge with it, and feel safer, calmer, and more intentional in your day-to-day experience.

Change Your Language

When you worry and ruminate, you turn on the sympathetic nervous system, thus raising your arousal levels. The same thing happens when you feel excitement. That's why the research of Alison Wood Brooks of Harvard Business School is interesting for anyone trying to stop worrying. She found that when you stop trying to control your nervous energy, and instead allow it to flow through you and even call it something more positive, you have the ability to manage it better.[3] It is normal to feel a surge of nervous excitement, for example, when speaking in front of a group of people. Rather than avoiding it or stifling the feeling, though, which makes it more pronounced, imagine a wave flowing through you.

As you mentally step to the other side where you feel more comfortable, you will relax. Instead of stifling your nervousness, tell yourself, "I am excited," or urge yourself to get excited. This strategy is not about trying to persuade yourself that things are easy when you know they're not, but about changing your threat mindset to a challenge mindset.

Warm Up to Calm Down

Believe it or not, another way to calm your worry is to warm your hands. Did you know you can actually increase blood flow to your hands?

When you're stressed, blood leaves the extremities and pools in the center of the body. That's why you get cold hands when you're scared or upset. By using your home thermometer as a feedback tool to measure your finger temperature instead of body temperature, you can learn to activate a relaxation response that changes your mental state from anxious and upset to calm, focused, and comfortable. In other words, by moving from Beta to Alpha.

Here's what you do: Take your baseline finger temperature first by attaching your index finger to the end of a thermometer with a piece of tape. Wait about 30 seconds and write down your finger temperature.

Now begin to think about your hands warming. You may want to imagine being at the beach or standing in front of a fireplace. Or just imagine your blood flowing down the arm into the hand. You might sense a little vibration or tingling. Moving the blood from the center of your body to your extremities stimulates your Alpha, or relaxation frequency. If you take your finger temperature again, you'll probably find that it has increased by one to two degrees or more. Any temperature in excess of 90 means you are really relaxed.

You may ask, why not just rub your hands together? Because warming your hands with this exercise shows you how powerful you are. And when you begin to understand the power of your mind, your self-confidence grows in other areas. If you can do this, what else can you accomplish?

The process of warming your hands also slows your breathing. This is good to know because often we're told that if we just breathe more slowly or deeper we can calm ourselves, but many times it is easier to raise the temperature in our hands than it is to change our breathing. This exercise is a nice preliminary to our next tool for eliminating worry: bilateral stimulation.

Bilateral Stimulation, or Walk for a Change

Use this next exercise when you feel really worried. Normally our mind resolves our negative emotions—worry, sadness, guilt—while we sleep. REM (rapid eye movement) action tends to reprocess our negative experience and place it in long-term memory, where it doesn't hurt as much to think about. Interestingly, this innate healing process that occurs for most of us in sleep can also occur through any bilateral movement you engage in, such as walking or hand tapping.[4] When you walk with your focus on the scenery and your rhythmic pace, and let yourself enter a meditative state, your brain produces Alpha. These brain waves are what stimulate interesting thoughts and ideas to pop into your head. You may enter a natural relaxed trance state where time slows, and you are less aware of the list of "must do items" you've made for the day. It is a simple but powerful tool that disrupts and diffuses anxiety by stimulating blood flow and electrical activity on both sides of the brain. That's why so many people feel better after exercising and why doctors recommend walking to lower stress.

Walking is particularly healing. It stimulates hemispheric balance by equalizing blood flow in both sides of the brain. When you are upset, the left hemisphere where rational processing occurs slams shut. The bilateral stimulation of walking, however, unlocks the right side of the brain and allows us to process our emotions. When you walk for 10 to 20 minutes and shift your attention away from a problem at the same time, your worry usually disappears, your anger floats away, and you can put yourself in a calm state. Who wouldn't want that? And it's free![5]

Instead of walking, sit and move your eyes back and forth. The actual side-to-side eye movement replicates REM action. You can use a ball that you toss from hand to hand while you track the movement from side to side, and you can quickly calm your nervous system. Your problems don't go away, but your intense feelings about them do, which puts you in a better frame of mind to solve it or decide it isn't a problem after all.

Any repetitive bilateral movement like patting your knees one at a time or drumming can have the same effect. Some of our clients have even tapped their hands alternately on the steering wheel while driving. Be sure to keep hold of the steering wheel while you do this exercise. When sitting down, you could even just take two fingers and move them back and forth at eye level.[6]

Try It Now

This is a simple three-minute exercise. You'll need a tennis ball, apple, or other small round object you can easily pass between your hands. Think about something that's worrying you and rate its effect on you on a scale of 1 to 10, with 10 being the worst, most debilitating feeling, and 1 being almost unnoticeable. Take the ball and gently toss it from hand to hand across the midline of the body six to eight times. Pause and check in with yourself: What number are you now? Keep doing the same exercise until you are a 1. Recheck whether the worry stays away by thinking again about the problem. If you feel your worry go up, go back and toss the ball again until you can remain at a one. This tool also alleviates pain and physical discomfort. You can do this exercise every time you find yourself worrying or obsessing over things that might go wrong. Once the worry decreases, try to figure out what the real issue is and move into an Alpha state to help you problem-solve.

Strike a Pose

When you shift your posture or stand in a confident way, you shift your mental state. Social psychologist Amy Cuddy discovered that when you change your physiology and stand in the "power pose" (imagine Wonder Woman with her hands on her hips), you activate feelings of confidence and certainty.[7] This pose is a great thing to do right before a talk or performance of any kind, including at work. When you stand up straight and take up more space, your personal power increases. Physiologically, the body begins to produce more testosterone and less cortisol. This chemical shift makes you feel less vulnerable and more powerful. But you can accomplish the same thing just by *imagining* yourself as Wonder Woman or your own favorite superhero, because imagining ourselves to be strong and powerful can actually make us more strong and powerful. Why? Because it shifts our brain waves from Beta to Alpha.

This does not mean you should go to your next meeting dressed in Spandex and a red cape. What it does mean is that if you train your brain to put itself in a superhero mindset, your mood, emotions, and even your body will reflect some of that superhero's confidence and strengths. By engaging in certain imaginary activities, you activate certain thought and neural patterns, and over time those thought patterns become second nature.

If none of these five exercises help you shake off your chronic worry, you may need to see a specialist. A combination of psychotherapy and neurofeedback can help you learn to relax and resolve issues that you may not even be aware of yet that perpetuate your worry. If you have difficulty relaxing, biofeedback can teach you this important skill.

In Summary

You can change mental states in a variety of ways. You can change your:

1. Physiology: When you shift your posture or stand in a confident way, you shift your mental state.
2. Language: By changing the words you use. Instead of, "I can't learn to play the piano," try changing it to "I choose not to learn to play the piano." Instead of "I can't stop myself from overeating," you could say, "I always choose what to put in my mouth."

3. Level of Arousal: If you are anxious and make impulsive decisions, focus on changing your internal worry state by calming the mind. If you are slow to get off the couch, set up a reward for going to the gym (this can't be donuts).

4. Mental Imagery: Imagine yourself in the mental state you want to experience. Remember a time you felt that way yourself and go over the details.

Power Thought: *You have more control over your thoughts and emotions than you ever imagined.*

———————

Now you have discovered tools that put you into a more balanced state. By doing these exercises, you demonstrate just how much control you have over your physiology. Changing your physiology allows you to manage your thoughts, mental states, and behaviors. In the next chapter we will discuss how you can use a brain change tool called Mind Wandering to launch your mind into Alpha, thus accessing the most creative ideas and solutions you can imagine.

CHAPTER 3

Zone Out to Make Big Decisions

Worry compounds the futility of being trapped on
a dead-end street. Thinking opens new avenues.
—Cullen Hightower

After six years as a struggling startup, Laura's small business
was finally taking off. In fact, she was doing so well her larg-
est competitor made an offer to buy her out. "Take the money and
run," her accountant told her, but her best friend said, "You've
come so far! How can you abandon your brain child?" It was a
huge decision with potential for significant rewards—or regrets—
on both sides. Laura felt paralyzed, and worrying about the pros

and cons of her options was sucking the joy out of what should have been a great moment in her life.

When Laura came to us, she said she needed to feel confident in order to make her important decision. We told her what we told you in Chapter 2, that our brains remember where we experience our emotions, so in order to regain her confidence she'd need to retrieve a memory about a time when she felt good about herself and a decision she had made. Remembering the experience in sensory detail would bring back the confident feeling she needed now. Ironically, the way to figure out a solution to her problem would be to take a break from trying to figure out a solution to her problem. We wanted her to try using a short-term tool that would activate her unconscious, where we knew lay all her forgotten confidence. This brief tool only takes five minutes, but can have extraordinary results.

The tool is called Mind Wandering. You might call it zoning out. To benefit from it, all you have to do is relax and allow your mind to visit pleasant scenes and landscapes either you have visited in person or seen in photographs. The reasons it works is that the best solutions come from a relaxed mind producing Alpha brain waves, not from a worried brain stressed with lots of high Beta. Too high Beta stimulates our limbic system, which triggers our protective flight-fight-freeze response. Alpha, however, allows the prefrontal cortex, which is the part of the brain responsible for executive function, to have clear thinking, impulse control, and the ability to delay gratification. When those systems are in play, we don't feel worried. We wanted Laura to use Mind Wandering to calm her limbic system and allow her prefrontal cortex to function well.

Beta is great for helping you make quick decisions, but Alpha is what you need to make the kind of important decisions that often require more thought. When you allow your mind to wander to positive images and memories, your slower frequencies of Alpha rise, the mind calms down, and you open the door to your unconscious. This is the part of the mind where we make new connections, find novel ideas, and develop our intuitions. A calm mind has the ability to evaluate options, see the bigger picture, and identify what we want and need. Trying to do that process in high Beta elevates our stress. Mind Wandering in Alpha, however, will actually trigger your creative mind to help you develop many solutions. The process takes you out of a dualistic category of a yes-no decision and into a world of other possibilities. Often, Alpha bursts just before you have an insight that gives you new direction and perspective. This burst, called an Alpha blink, temporarily shuts off the visual input to the brain so your creativity rises. The best entrepreneurs have been found to live in more Alpha. It's the juice that produces novel thinking.

Focusing away from a problem and shifting into Alpha gives you access to your unconscious, in which many worry-reducing resources reside. One of these resources is something we call a mosaic decision-constructing process, where you look at a situation from many different perspectives. If you can get your conscious mind to linger in a pleasant state, you'll give your unconscious mind a chance to actively try to answer your question about which path is the best. When you're worried, your unconscious mind works more effectively than your conscious mind. That's why so often we have our eureka moments in the shower or while going for a run; we're relaxed, which allows our conscious mind to back away from the thing that's stressing us out, giving our unconscious—where everything we have learned and every experience we've had has been recorded to become a potential source of help—a chance to look through the mosaic of possible solutions and find the best one.

Per our instructions, Laura went home that day and sat down on her bed. She allowed her mind to wander to the day she graduated from college. She had been so proud of herself. Then she remembered the time she was accepted by two MBA programs, and how she had struggled over which would be the best fit for her. One was more prestigious, and one offered a scholarship. She remembered that once she had realized there was no wrong choice, she had been able to quickly make up her mind. There had been power in making that decision, dealing with the consequences, moving forward, and not looking back with regret.

And there was more. After completing her MBA she could have followed her friends into a big job with a management firm, but after a great deal of deliberation she had decided to take a different path and strike out as an entrepreneur. As she sat on her bed, she remembered how empowered she had felt when starting her business and how prepared she was to deal with the unique set of problems she knew would accompany this endeavor. Once she started, she never looked back. Suddenly, her current dilemma looked much more manageable. When she gathered all the data, she realized there was no wrong choice. Either decision would take her on a slightly different trajectory, but the upsides were all in her favor. She could live with the consequences, whatever they were. In that frame of mind, she lost all her fear, and happily called her competitor to reject the offer.

The Importance of Daydreams

Psychiatrist Milton Erickson liked to tell a story about the disappearing manuscript. He was struggling to finish a book. His publisher was pressuring him to turn in the manuscript, but he didn't feel it was finished. The pressure was stressing him out. One day he took the manuscript with him to his desk and sat down to work. But after trying to write for about an hour, he felt himself getting tired, and allowed himself to slip into a daydream. Some time later, he came to, but when he looked back down at his desk, he couldn't find the manuscript. (Remember: This was during a time when you couldn't just open your computer and print out a new copy, so losing a manuscript was problematic.) He didn't panic, though. Instead he tried to put the manuscript, and the stress it was causing him, out of his mind. A couple of weeks later, he came back to his desk chair, relaxed, and found the manuscript under some papers that he must have absent mindedly placed over it.

Lots of people find lost objects sitting in plain sight, but Milton Erickson had a reason to believe that his unconscious mind might have deliberately led him to daydream and cover the manuscript. Erickson overcame numerous handicaps, including paralysis from polio, which almost killed him. He learned to walk again by watching his baby sister learn to walk. He observed her minute muscle movements and used mental rehearsal while in trance states to stimulate his own neural muscular pathways. Erickson learned that the memory of how to walk resided in his unconscious, and after this amazing achievement, he always trusted that his unconscious mind would hold any solution or wisdom he needed.

Once Erickson became a professional psychiatrist, he'd use the story about his manuscript to illustrate that we often don't know what we know. His unconscious mind knew he wasn't ready to turn the book in, so it had given him the time to mentally work out the parts with which he was struggling. That's why he didn't panic: He was sure that once he'd shifted his attention so he could get into a more relaxed state, he would figure out what he wanted to say, and his mind would allow him to find the pages. And it did.[1]

Our attention is affected by the ultradian rhythm that alters our attention span every 90 to 120 minutes throughout the day. Mind Wandering naturally occurs at the end of this cycle, as well as after any intense cognitive task. Introducing the slower Alpha brain waves that allow Mind Wandering is our mind's way of forcing us to give it a rest. Sometimes we can get so lost in our Mind Wandering that we go into a trance, otherwise known as a daydream, a more intense version of Mind Wandering.

Daydreams are wonderful for spurring problem-solving: When you're daydreaming, you're in a trance state that combines internally focused attention with memory and imagination. It's a state of mind that gives you permission to connect to your own creativity free from self-criticism. At times you may even wander into "Walter Mitty" daydreams that feel extraordinarily real and allow you to enjoy experiences that your conscious mind would normally censor or dismiss as impossible. In your daydreams, you might be visiting a foreign land when you meet your soul mate. The connection is so strong it makes you feel more alive than you have in a long time. A daydream this powerful could compel you to think hard about your inner yearnings and wonder if all of your needs are being met in your current relationship.

If worry and anxiety are blocking you from solving a problem, you could try a method suggested in 1911 by William James, known as the father of American psychology. He called it "nonthinking." You do it like this: Set a goal and "unclamp" from the outcome—just allow any ideas about how you might achieve the goal to surface and write them down without analyzing them, even if they seem preposterous. Then you let them simmer in the back of your mind to see if they would be the best problem-solving approaches. The point of the exercise is not actually to achieve the goal, but to stimulate creative thought. Without knowing James, several important thought leaders throughout history have used a similar process to open up their minds. Einstein performed thought experiments where he daydreamed running beside a light beam to the edge of the universe. He credited this creative endeavor for helping him develop the theory of relativity. Another thinker, Isaac Newton, found that allowing his mind to wander resulted in clear thinking and problem-solving, and ultimately led him to develop the theory of gravity. Even Thomas Edison, who developed more than 1,000 patents for inventions, would sit in his chair holding steel balls. He relaxed deeply and when his hands dropped the balls, he woke up and wrote down his ideas.

A study done at the University of California, Santa Barbara, found that when people took a break from worrying about a problem and focused on something less taxing, their performance increased by 40 percent.[2] In fact, when you are feeling stressed about an issue, stop thinking about it and do something relaxing. There comes a time of diminishing returns to continue to try to come up with solutions. When the mind fatigues, it's time to make a change. Take your mind completely away from a problem or take a nap. Though you change your mental state and focus of attention, your unconscious mind continues to work on the problem. This approach often triggers a eureka moment.

You can use Mind Wandering to help you solve long-term big-picture projects, but you can also use it strategically to keep you performing your best at work every day. Give your cognitive process a five-minute break every 45 minutes by focusing on a lovely vacation or experience from your past. Inspired by how well she had used attention shifting to regain her confident mindset, Laura began to take five minutes here and there and let her mind wander to her favorite place, Maui. She loved the gentle breeze, the beauty of the islands, the blue water, and especially how relaxed she felt when she was there. After about a week of this positive Mind Wandering, she found that she was getting better at solving problems at work. It was as though the pressure and speed of her daily existence just couldn't rattle her anymore.

Divergent Thinking

Mind Wandering is linked to what is called "divergent thinking," a thought process that generates many solutions to a problem. Divergent thinking allows you to see beyond self-imposed limitations and keeps you open to experience. It often occurs after a period of Mind Wandering on unrelated things or pleasant past experiences. Divergent thinkers often see connections where others cannot, and this difference in perception leads toward novel ideas.

You may feel at your most creative after a period of positive Mind Wandering. It is often at this point when we say our muse has touched us, when our inspiration and creative output accelerates. We could "muse" that highly focused attention doesn't accomplish everything for us. Researchers at the University of California, Santa Barbara, discovered that our natural state might be a combination of external focus followed by inward exploration. They said, "Consciousness is continuously moving with ever-changing content, but also ebbs like a breaking wave, outwardly expanding and then inwardly retreating."[3] Positive and constructive Mind Wandering can have many positive returns. In particular, it can teach you how to think outside your own box.

Caution: Don't Get Lost

It's easy to get lost in our daydreams, and zoning out too often is not productive. If you've got a day left to complete a statistical report for work and you're taking five-minute daydream breaks every half hour, you're going to run into trouble. And if you zone out while driving, you may cut your future short. Time and place matter.

Mind Wanderings to avoid:

1. Distracted Mind Wandering. It is possible to allow your mind to wander too much. Recently society has started labeling individuals with chronically wandering minds as Attention Deficit Disorder. In the past, having ADD was an asset. Early hunters

would have benefited from the ability to notice multiple small disturbances in a field or forest. Their hyper-alert brains would have made it easier for them to react quickly and find their prey than their more methodical, single-track kin. Unfortunately, that kind of mind isn't so well suited for today's school settings, and it can be disastrous in the workplace; there are so many digital distractions to keep you from completing simple tasks.

If you have trouble focusing and are Mind Wandering too much, try the following exercise.

Look out your window at the houses or apartment buildings across from yours and count the panes of glass you see in the windows. Notice their pattern and symmetry. How many windows do you see? As you count, stay aware of how your focus becomes heightened and clear when you do this. How long can you keep this up before boredom becomes a daydream? Practice a bit and each time see how much longer you can stay with it. What else could you count? Counting makes the brain focus on one thing that isn't difficult to accomplish. Performing the exercise regularly builds connections to the prefrontal cortex, which will increase your ability to stay with a task.

2. Revenge Mind Wandering. Sometimes when we're frustrated or angry we get stuck imagining the way a conversation *should* have gone, or we plot out every word of the conversation we will have one day if we ever get the chance. Spending time in mental fights temporarily relieves tension but is ultimately unproductive. For example, it would be normal to feel angry, upset, powerless, and sad after a layoff. You might really relish imagining a version of your final meeting with HR where instead of silently leaving the office to pack your stuff, you interrupt that smug HR manager with a screed against corporate tyranny. But unless you can shift out of your sense of outrage and do what it takes to get another job and regain your security and safety, you can get stuck in a limbic system freeze. If you do it too much you can put yourself in a defensive and adversarial mindset. The conversations can feel so real they can make your pulse race faster or your stomach churn as you hurl a perfect zinger that puts your adversaries in their place. Your brain might go offline for a while and you may spend an inordinate amount of time ruminating over

everything you wish you had said or done to those who wronged you. But that kind of Mind Wandering wastes your energy. You have to shift your perspective and allow the mind to wander into different viewpoints.

To shift perspective you must shift into Alpha and calm your limbic system. Get your feelings off your chest by expressing your agitation over being laid off to trusted friends. Go to the gym and exercise so you feel better physically. Then call your network and set up lunch dates for help in transitioning to some new job. Once you start to feel a little less emotional and angry, try this exercise to help you look at your changed circumstances from a different perspective.

Take three different chairs and position them in a triangle. Take a fourth chair and place it outside the triangle. Every chair represents a different perspective through which you can look at your situation. These are called perceptual positions.[4] In this exercise, the first position is your own perspective. If you sit here, you will see through your own eyes. Sit in the second position, and you'll take on the role of a colleague who listens and gives feedback and suggestions. The third perceptual position is that of an interested but distant observer like the company board member; from this position you can observe the dynamics occurring between the first two positions. Finally, the fourth position sits away from the other three, and notices how the entire system is operating and whether it's working or not.

By placing yourself in all four positions, you can glean different understandings of your circumstances from four different perspectives. Perspective-taking gives you a sense of how others perceive things and can help you get the distance you need to go forward.

Let's continue with the example that you've been laid off. To start gaining a new perspective, you'd sit in the first chair and verbalize your understanding of what has happened to you. Go ahead and vent. Self-pity is okay here. You might say, "I worked so hard to develop that program and this is how they repay me? Let's see how far they get without me. They don't know what they're losing. I thought I would stay in this position for 20 years. I am angry and sad and deeply disappointed. I believe my career is over." This is the "I" position.

Now, move to position two, and have a conversation with yourself over in first position. Remember: You're a colleague now, so your job is to be empathic, but offer a different perspective. You might say, "I see you're struggling and upset. This is a career you thought was your life's purpose. I understand it is really difficult to imagine doing anything else. It may be that you are better suited in a different role and you would be happier doing something else." This is the "you" position.

Now move back to the first chair and respond to the second position. You may want to go back and forth in conversation for a while until you feel a bit more settled and relieved of the internal tension around your upset feelings. Eventually, you will feel calmer.

Once you feel calm, move to the third chair and imagine you are an external consultant with no knowledge about what has happened. In this third position you make no judgments but are curious about the dilemma. For example, you might say from the third position, "I can see that You 1 (you in first position) are really unhappy and You 2 (you in second position) are wondering what could help." Then you might ask yourself (You 3), "Do you have an idea of what you are passionate about, what your dream job might be?" Once you are honest with yourself you can move into creating a new future.

Finally, go sit in the fourth chair outside of the triangle. This is the "we" position. From this perspective of being able to see the whole context and entire system, say aloud the most positive future you can imagine. You might say, "As we look together toward our best future and acknowledge what is really true, we can decide if our strengths and potentials work together toward creating success for everyone." Use this fourth perspective to develop a plan of action. Use your imagination to try to see other options and new directions that might be even better and more fun than the situation you just left. By the time you see your situation from the fourth position, your worry and upset will have dissipated, and you will know yourself better.

In doing this exercise, you calm the limbic system and begin to operate from the prefrontal cortex. By trying to see a situation from a different perspective, you free yourself from the prison of your own limiting ideas and feelings. After this exercise, take a rest and let your mind wander and imagine different futures. Avoid coming up with potential obstacles and just wander around in reverie. Think about your passions and hobbies. Would you be happy if you just did those all day, every day? Imagine that you can. Don't stop yourself with "That's silly." Just imagine it. Once you overcome the negative Mind Wandering, your mind is free to develop innovative and practical strategies to accomplish these dreams.

Mindfulness Meditation

You can overdo Mind Wandering, in which case you become so removed from life you get stuck by inertia. But Mind Wandering that never brings you new solutions is useless. Practicing mindfulness meditation, however, can interrupt the stressful loop that swings you from hyperfocus to unproductive mind wanderings and calms rumination.

Richard Davidson at University of Wisconsin Medical School in Madison, Wisconsin, discovered that meditation leads to a reduction of electrical and metabolic activity in the amygdala, which when overactivated is associated with worry. The most recent research found that meditation creates self-regulation in 11 hours of training.[5] The practice of meditation helps people appropriately regulate their emotions. As a result, they are less emotionally reactive and less emotionally constricted. They are better able to handle stressful situations. Mindfulness meditation begins with the simple task of sitting and focusing on your breath or walking and being aware of your body's movement. Another way to meditate is through walking meditation. Pay close attention to the movement of your body as you walk slowly and let go of thoughts. This is different from bilateral stimulation in that the focus of meditation is to just notice where and how you take steps and be present in the moment rather than trying to move your eyes back and forth. The process of meditation allows you to let go of judgment and grasping after things, and to be fully aware in the here and now. In both instances, the discipline of mindfulness begins with the calming of the mind. These exercises help you become better at controlling when you want your mind to drift and when you want it to pay attention. Narrowly focusing on a problem or letting the mind wander becomes a choice rather than obsessive thinking, worry, or distraction. Mindfulness meditation can be a tool that actually puts you in charge of your life, so you decide when to focus your attention on a problem and when you allow yourself to go into creative Mind Wandering.

Try It Now

Get a timer and set it for five minutes. Find a comfortable chair and sit in it with your feet on the ground, your back supported by the chair, and relax your shoulders. Allow your head to balance on your neck so your head is still but relaxed. Moving only your eyes, look toward the floor about 3 feet in front of you, keeping a soft gaze. Allow your body to relax, supported by the floor and the chair. Place your hands on your lap and begin focusing on your breath. Allow yourself to breathe naturally. Some breaths may be long; some may be short. Just notice your breathing, don't try to control it. Silently count your exhalations. Each breath should receive a number. First breath = 1; second breath = 2; and so on, until you reach 5. And then begin again.

Any time your mind wanders and you notice it, say to yourself silently the word *thinking*, and return to counting your exhalations. When your timer goes off, stop the meditation. Do this every day at approximately the same time. If after a week you want to extend the time, add a minute. The gradual increase in time will seem manageable. It is better to do this every day than just once in a while or only when you are stressed. You may notice as you meditate for longer periods of time that the more you practice letting go of your thoughts, the easier it becomes to let go of self-critical, self-blaming thinking, rumination, and revenge fantasies. Whether you practice letting go of thinking or hitting a golf ball, the more you practice, the easier it becomes over time, and the better you become. It is a skill like any other, requiring practice. Eventually skilled meditators don't need to count their breaths. They simply notice what is happening in a nonreactive and deattached attitude.

Meditation is a way of accessing the mental state you need to be in to observe problems from different perceptual positions. All of the exercises in this chapter are designed to help you get unstuck from problematic thinking, which comes from being tied to a particular perceptual position, and locked into high Beta brain activity. Once unstuck, you can be free from worry.

To Dream Is to Build a Future

Harvard psychologists Daniel Gilbert and Matthew Killingsworth discovered that generally people's minds wander 46.9 percent of the time except during sex (well, unless you're bored with the activity).[6] This means that nearly half of your life is spent daydreaming.

Daydreaming builds strength in the prefrontal cortex by stimulating more neural connections. The more you visit potential positive futures, the more opportunities you have to evaluate whether they will get you there.

Mental Time Travel

Haven't you ever wished you could go back in time and tell your younger self what you know now? The following exercise lets you do the next best thing.

Neuroscience studies show that each time we review the past, we rework the memory so it is reconsolidated differently, and the brain stores it as a slightly changed memory. When you decharge a negative memory, you dissolve the trauma and are able to see the experience from a larger perspective. You can be aware that you survived even though there was loss and there is a reason to go forward. Free from the grasp that the trauma holds, often you can become aware of external and internal resources of which you might have been unaware. When you review positive memories, you can use those resourceful states accompanying them in the present for problem resolution. Each memory also serves as a blueprint for future actions. So occasionally reviewing the past helps us construct the future we want to walk into. When the memory is pleasant and focused on past successes, the experiences create a good internal resource upon which to build your best future.

Try It Now

Relax your body and mind. Think about your most successful self five years in the future. Consider where you are living and how you are dressed. Mind Wander to this place in the future and have a conversation with your future wiser self. Listen to what advice your future self might give you.

Now let's look at how contagious other people's worries are.

Can You Pick Up Other People's Worry?

Whenever you feel empathy, you in fact are imagining another person's emotional state. You are, metaphorically, in another person's mind, and it is possible to feel their worry. In fact, your brain is picking up their brain waves. Do you ever cry at movies? It's an example of visiting that character's mind. Emotions can be contagious. When you are around someone who worries a lot, it is easy to get caught up in their worry and limited thinking, and begin to believe that there are no solutions to their problems or even your own. You can protect yourself from getting caught up in their emotional turmoil by noticing your own thinking and assumptions. But you can engage in intentional Group Mind Wandering when everyone is on the same page.

Group Zone Out

Positive zoning out is a great thing to do. Do it in a group, and it can be even greater. This activity is different from brainstorming in that the entire group goes into a trance state for 10 to 20 minutes before offering any new ideas. Most people find that

Mind Wandering together stimulates more creative ideas more frequently than if you are alone. As long as your motivation is to work together, this group mind emerges with a work team, a family, a couple, or even a singing organization.

A group of paper clips that are close to a magnet will jump a gap and connect to the magnet through the magnetic field produced between them. In a similar fashion, a group of human minds interacts to create new associations that might not otherwise occur.

Through asking positive questions about what is possible for the future and how best to get there, no person in the group falls into worry. The shared positive mental state allows group members to blend as if they were a flock of birds flying in formation, silently communicating and moving together to get to their intended destination.

Moments After Mind Wandering

We often feel clear, calm, and connected after a round of positive Mind Wandering because it clears us for a while of our habitual attention style, mental models, and old patterns, and allows us to see things from a more expanded view that perceives our infinite potential and our connection to the rest of the world. When you move out of conditioned thinking and into the realm of possibility, it's harder to return to a state of worry.

In this almost sacred and brief time right after Mind Wandering, ask yourself, "What do I want? What matters to me? What lights up my life?" Rather than focusing as usual on what others want or expect from you, focus on your deep yearnings. Is there something you really want to do? Try to hold yourself in a place of openness for a while and don't allow your mind to start telling you why you can't do things.

If you have difficulty doing this, sit in front of a tree for 20 minutes and allow your mind to wander around the details of the tree. Notice the amazing symmetry of the leaves and the patterns of the veins in the leaves. Observe the wind blowing through the tree and the pleasant sound the tree makes in response. You'll find yourself in a relaxed state. Then ask the previous questions and see what answers you find.

Decision by Mind Wandering

Even though it seems contradictory, decisions made by Mind Wandering are often just as effective as those made through deliberate consideration. Colleen Giblin of the Tepper School of Business, Carey Morewedge, and Michael Norton of Carnegie Mellon University conducted experiments in which participants judged the value of a randomly chosen art poster through conscious deliberation, Mind Wandering, or random assignment. The researchers predicted that participants would like the art poster they deliberately chose the most and the one their minds settled on from Mind Wandering the least. The researchers discovered, however, that the opposite was true.[7] The results mean that our unconscious mind is so smart, it can make a decision better if you allow the mind to move into Alpha relaxation rather than struggling consciously.

Yawning Regulates Your Attention

One more wonderful activity that can enhance Mind Wandering is yawning. Most of the time we try to stifle our yawns (go ahead and try it now). Yet yawning dissolves worry, turns down cortisol, and activates a neural pathway to empathy. When you yawn, your frontal lobe quiets, which lets your mind wander and calm down, decreasing your feelings of worry. So go ahead—yawn, relax, and yawn again.

Power Thought: When you put worry on hold and let your mind wander, you can solve any problem, break persistent habits, develop your intuition, and devise better plans for the future.

You are becoming aware of how important it is to Mind Wander strategically to restore your energy and reset your mind. Turn to daydreams to help you rest, receive creative ideas, and enhance your intuition. In the next chapter we will explore a powerful tool that settles the mind for several days at a time.

PART II

The Brain's Super Powers

CHAPTER 4

Deep State Dive to Dissolve Worry and Rumination

We can easily manage if we will only take,
each day, the burden appointed to it.

—John Newton

Evelyn was late to work. Again. She couldn't explain it. Every day she set her alarm with plenty of time to get dressed, eat breakfast, and drive the 5 miles to her job located in a bland corporate office park in the Woodlands, just north of Houston. And every day, she was at least 30 minutes late, even when she set her alarm a half hour earlier. This time, though, the minute she slid behind her desk and started up her computer, a chat box popped up on the bottom of her screen. It was from her boss, Mark, and its brevity was ominous: Please come to my office.

The meeting with Mark was almost as brief. Evelyn was informed that she was on probation for 30 days. If she couldn't be on time every day for that month, she would be fired. As Evelyn trudged back to her desk, she had no doubt her boss hoped she would fail. She was sure he and her colleagues would like nothing more than to be rid of her. What a shame, she thought sarcastically. They had to go through all the paperwork and documentation before they could kick her to the curb, unlike her ex-boyfriend who had simply texted her the day after Valentine's Day to say, "I can't do this anymore. Sorry." She opened up her desk drawer and pulled out a jumbo-sized box of Junior Mints, popping a large handful into her mouth. What was another pound when she'd already put on 20 in the last six months? She chewed hard, hoping that the intense cold sweetness and exaggerated motion of her jaws would help keep her from crying where everyone could see.

Evelyn came to see us for the first time shortly after getting her boss's ultimatum. We asked her to walk us through her morning ritual to help us figure out what was slowing her down before she could get out the door. We noticed that she interspersed her description of her actions—getting out of bed, taking a shower, picking out her clothes—with a number of negative asides about her job, calling it everything from "stupid" to "dumb" to "pointless." It didn't take much prodding to get her to admit that she was utterly unfulfilled by her work but was afraid to leave because she didn't think her boss would give her a good recommendation. "Because of your tardiness?" we asked. No, that was the least of it. Her relationship with her boss and most of her colleagues had been strained long before she started having trouble making it to work on time. She held a lot of responsibility, but they apparently didn't like the fact that she didn't just smile and shrug her shoulders when they refused her repeated requests for more help. To prepare herself better for the challenges of her day, every morning she would mentally check off every troublesome task and project she knew she would face and try to figure out how she was going to handle it.

Her worry that she was going to fail meant that by the time she got to the office, her tension was so high she had started craving the cigarettes she'd quit a decade earlier. After her breakup, her negative thoughts about work were compounded by her grief as she indulged in vengeful thoughts against her ex-boyfriend. She often vacillated between feeling tired and numb or combative and angry, but found that sinking her teeth into a soft, oversized coffee chocolate-chip muffin from the office cafeteria often calmed her nerves. Come to think of it, she craved carbs all the time lately. She knew that medicating her feelings with baked goods and fast food was what had caused her rapid weight gain, but eating felt like the only pleasure she had left. She was disgusted with herself.

Visiting us was not the first time Evelyn had made an effort to turn her life around. She had read self-help books and tried to change her negative thinking patterns, she had explored her past in therapy, she had started taking yoga at the local gym. But still she constantly felt like the little old lady in the long-running Discount Tire Company television commercial, ready to hurl a tire through a plate glass window. "It is what it is," she often said in morose tone.

A little worry can be helpful, lighting a fire under us to motivate us to start on a task. But too much hijacks our brains. It was obvious to us that Evelyn was in limbic-system overdrive. Her morning ritual of trying to get a grip on her day and problem-solve ahead of time was keeping her stuck in a flight-fight-freeze mode and training her mind to stay in a permanently worried state, which was raising her arousal levels and causing her to snap at her boss and coworkers, as well as seek out the soothing comfort of fat, sugar, and salt. She desperately needed to reset her neural circuits.

Evelyn had good reason to be unhappy, but she—not the job, not the boss, and not the boyfriend—was responsible for putting herself into such a negative state of mind. The good news was that this meant she was wholly capable of getting herself out of it. To do so, she had to begin identifying what she was doing to heighten her worry to such extreme levels. We identified three different culprits: a stress mindset, a stress generator, and stress overload. Let's look at these in greater detail.

Stress Mindset

A study published by Yale psychologist Alia Crum found that a stress mindset—the mental "frame" or "lens" that you use when you approach and understand an experience—makes all the difference in whether you worry or you don't.[1] If you have a negative stress mindset, you believe that stress saps your energy and inhibits your ability to grow, and that therefore you should avoid stress at all costs. If your stress mindset is positive, however, you feel that it makes you healthier and enhances both your performance and productivity.

Crum and her colleagues found that people with a positive stress mindset were better able to handle stress. They were more likely to ask for feedback on their performance, whether at work or in other contexts, and absorb it in a constructive way.

Unfortunately, Evelyn suffered from a negative stress mindset. And there was more.

Stress Generator

According to the "stress generator" hypothesis, people play an active role in creating their own stressful life events by virtue of the way they handle their everyday situations. In other words, a negative approach to life generates more stress, and a positive approach generates less. Someone who generates stress for themselves might have an "Eeyore Syndrome." Eeyore is the sad donkey in *Winnie the Pooh*. On a sunny day, he might say, "I'll probably get burned"; on a rainy day, he'd grumble, "My lunch will get soggy." Evelyn was getting close to developing a full-blown Eeyore Syndrome. She didn't know how to hold on to the enjoyable experiences she had. Even when pleasant things happened to her, it was difficult for her to appreciate them. She could only notice what was wrong and imagine everything that might go wrong in the future. Her boss's and colleagues' negative reactions to her chronic tardiness and hostile attitude reinforced her negative outlook. "They don't understand me," she thought. "I'll probably get burned."

There are three consequences to allowing your feelings of stress to dominate your interactions with others. First, it can cause you to overlook the support they offer you. When people feel unacknowledged when they try to support you, they eventually become tired and pull away. Second, when you can't acknowledge other people's support, your emotional batteries lose energy and you may withdraw. Third, all the worry that stems from stress can cause a secondary depression, which can lead you to develop avoidance strategies. We suspected all three consequences were derailing Evelyn's life. Were her boss and coworkers really that critical, or was everyone caught in a feedback loop of action and reaction? Even a little pessimism will increase the negativity in yourself and those around you. Negativity eventually triggers anger, which interferes with your ability to make great decisions. After a while, you may not even recognize that you feel anger: It just becomes your normal default state, as natural as breathing.

Stress Overload

If you live in daily stress and finally plunge over your stress threshold, you dramatically reduce your prefrontal cognitive abilities. Worse yet, prolonged stress changes the structure of this part of the brain. Because the prefrontal cortex regulates our thoughts, behaviors, and feelings through neural connections with other brain areas, it also helps us correct our perceptions and decisions when needed. If those neural connections begin to wither due to stress overload, these important corrective functions are compromised, leaving us incapable of changing our minds or recalibrating our feelings once a situation changes or we gather more information. Stress overload combined with an inability to hold positive feelings leads to personal and social handicaps that can prevent us from having a successful life.

But you can rewire your brain and learn how to avoid reactive responses by spending more time in what's called the liminal state. Liminal means "the space between," or the transition between one place, one state, or one thing and another. When the sun begins to set, you are in a liminal space watching the transition from day to night. When friends leave after a wonderful visit, their departure signals the transition between social engagement and being alone again. A little sadness accompanies the transition, and you must make a slight mental adjustment. When it comes to your brain, the liminal state is the transitional level between waking consciousness and sleep.

You'll recall from Chapter 1 that we generate Theta brain waves when we're drowsy and on the edge of falling asleep or waking up. In fact, the liminal state is just another term for the Theta state. This state is different than the one you're in when you're taking a nap. Though naps are regenerative and important, as is rest in general, the Theta state is a special and distinctive state from sleep. Theta triggers an endogenous relaxation healing process that may act as therapy for the limbic system, and it begins the process of associating new and more positive perceptions to events we call neuro-association. And Evelyn's limbic system sorely needed a break.

Neuro-association is based on the idea that we represent our experiences through images, feelings, smells, sounds, or a combination of these elements. This process can be useful and problematic. If the representations cause us pain, we can re-associate them by eliminating the emotional charge that may have been attached at the time we had the experience. For example, if your father was harsh and yelled at you, you may hear your partner "yelling" when he or she isn't even increasing the volume in speaking to you. In this case, the ability to distinguish the partner from the father is important in eliminating the reaction. Another more positive example is to picture these word images: waves, moon, sand, ocean, water. Now think of a laundry detergent. You may have come up with the names Tide or Surf laundry detergents and felt a sense of comfort if this brand is what you use. Your brain makes associations to the words.

The link between images or thoughts and emotions can unconsciously influence your behavior. These connections can make a difference in how much money you make, what kind of diet you eat, and what possibilities you believe in for your life.

For decades, researchers have known that putting people into a state of deep relaxation can help eliminate all kinds of problems related to worry such as weight, anxiety, depression, and physical pain. The deep state tends to de-charge the links to problems, and in profound relaxation, your mind moves into solutions you haven't thought about. You can achieve all of these positive changes without psychotherapy or biofeedback when you know how to practice what we call the deep state dive, which is basically holding yourself for long periods of time in the liminal state so that Theta can work its healing magic.

Why Theta Heals

Long lampooned as loopy accessories for the New Age crowd, flotation tanks, also known as isolation tanks, have actually long worked as excellent scientific testing grounds into the effects of restricted environmental stimulation (REST) and what happens when people gain access to their unconscious mind. Scientists in the 1980s wanted to know why people floating in a soundproof, skin-temperature bath of Epsom salt water, often while listening to piped-in meditation music, experienced dramatically improved psychological and physical wellness. In record time, people reported losing weight, decreased rheumatoid arthritis pain, vanishing worry, and increased happiness. Best of all, these startling changes lingered long after the flotation experience was over.

Why would immersing oneself in a flotation tank work more quickly than other therapy approaches? Relaxing in the flotation tank puts people in a Theta state. Remember: When you start to relax or go to sleep at night, your brain begins to produce more Alpha waves. As you deeply relax, your neural processes move into Theta and then later Delta for deeper sleep. These states of sleep are important to regenerate the brain, mind, and body. While in these states, the brain releases endocannabinoids that facilitate a "cleansing" and healing process. One of the main endocannabinoids released in the Theta state is anandamide, whose name derives from the Sanskrit word for "bliss." Anandamide diminishes stress and physical pain and produces wonderful feelings of well-being. In fact, anandamide has the same chemical structure as marijuana. Yes, that's right, your brain can get you stoned using its very own natural marijuana-like neurotransmitter. In the liminal state—Theta, in between the initial relaxation of Alpha and the deep sleep of Delta—through a process we don't quite understand yet, our brain's natural relaxation chemicals create such deep relaxation that the mind enters a profound quiet space. And in that quiet space, we often see dream images without being asleep. These are called hypnogogic imagery, and they tend to be vivid and transient. It is here when Theta is more dominant than the other brain-wave frequencies, and where healing can begin: "Deep relaxation places humans within a 'target zone' for the endogenous release of any of the family of neuropeptides of relaxation. The target zone is a state of Theta, sometimes referred to as a state of hypnogogic reverie, and it is the bull's-eye of the deep healing process."[2] When you access and stay in this state for 10 to 20 minutes—otherwise known as a deep state dive—the dream images that emerge can help point you to solutions to problems that plague your waking state. In fact, anandamide helps create more neural connections and uploads a huge increase in creativity, often by 700 percent.[3]

How Theta Heals Worry

The neuro-association process that occurs by hovering in Theta for a while allows you to automatically let go of worry, and to release mental baggage, those troubling thoughts, memories, and ruminations that have frozen your mind in the past. In Theta, fear dissipates, a problem transforms into a doable challenge, and it gives you the ability to tolerate life's trials more easily. It is where you find intuition, creative ideas, perceptions, insights, and deep awareness. Within Theta you find a deep pool of self-compassion and a calm, quiet center that "knows" everything will be all right, no matter the difficulty. Even if you have great worries much of the time, deep down beneath the worry resides that still space. You can find it when you access your deepest relaxed state.

A deep dive in the Theta state can help you begin to realize that a fixed reality is illusory. What does that mean? It means that no matter how convinced you are the world works a certain way, or that life is on a fixed path, change is always possible. In fact, your perception shifts to see new possibilities that you have not noticed before. When you're in that still, internal space, Theta provides guidance from the deepest level of your mind about which fork in the road to take, and how to move into the future you would like to experience.

Theta can help you access clarity in thinking. Without the overlay of worry, your ability to think outside the box you created expands. It's incredibly useful for when you're faced with a seemingly impossible goal. With broader and flexible thinking, you can tackle that goal even if you're not sure how you're going to get there. You'll also find it's hard to worry when you're approaching problems creatively; you're more likely to replace that worry with a sense of curiosity. Applying a new twist or perspective jolts lateral thinkers out of their habitual frame of reference and triggers novel solutions. For example, a choir wanted to fund a trip to sing in Europe. Although they had put on events before to raise money, including bake sales, they were rarely able to attract people outside of their own music circles to participate. Someone in the choir council who had tried several deep dive sessions for another unrelated problem started to think outside the box and came up with the idea to construct edible gingerbread houses that looked like old European castles. This novel idea enticed more people than ever before to purchase the desserts for the holidays, and the choir sold enough to pay for the trip.

Theta has also been shown to cure addictions. Drinking excessively, for example, is really a symptom of underlying stress or conflict, which causes worry. Worry hurts, and some people turn to alcohol, food, or other substances to medicate their pain. Addicts are seeking comfort; they use these substances to change their psychophysiological state. Unfortunately, the addictive cycle is extremely difficult to break. But not too long ago, Eugene Peniston, a psychologist from a Veterans Administration hospital in Colorado, decided to test a question: If Theta provides comfort to the brain, could it also provide comfort for chronic alcoholics?[4]

The statistics were grim: The relapse rate for alcohol and drug abuse programs was 80 percent after one year. In other words, a rehab program was considered a success if a mere 20 percent of patients who completed it were still sober after a year. Those alarming statistics reflect the power that chemical addiction has in making significant alterations in the brain and how the chemicals take away an individual's ability to provide self-comfort.

For his study, Peniston created two groups out of a selection of individuals who had been hospitalized for alcohol addiction. One group received only the hospital program; the other group received deep state dive training in addition to the hospital program.

Those alcoholics receiving deep state dive training were asked to do three things two times per day for 30 days: visualize themselves rejecting alcohol; use autogenic exercises, relaxation, and imagery techniques; and training in how to raise the temperature in their hands to trigger their relaxation (see Chapter 1 for instructions on raising temperature without biofeedback). Before the deep state dive experience, the men practiced warming their hands, and warming different areas in the body. During the deep state dive, the men visualized themselves rejecting the alcohol. Finally, the men trained on biofeedback machines to raise and condition their alpha and theta frequencies so their brains could restore the ability to provide self-comfort. Often, when people drink excessively or use drugs, their Alpha disappears and Beta rises, which makes them become anxious. Their normal reaction to this problem is to increase their alcohol intake, at which point the brain just gives up producing its own Alpha. By dipping down into Theta two times a day, the patients' brains normalized their ability to provide their own deep comfort—without the aid of outside substances.

Eighty percent of the men who received the deep state dive treatment remained sober five years after the study. Those who only received the hospital program had returned to drinking within a 36-month follow-up. Peniston literally turned the relapse numbers on their head. This study was replicated in Houston in 2005, measuring a larger number of people with poly addictions, and revealed similar results.[5]

This kind of treatment for alcohol and drug abuse is best done in a hospital with neurofeedback as part of the treatment, but the studies demonstrated the remarkable healing power of Theta on the brain, mind, and body.

Re-Programming With Theta

Our families, culture, and personal experiences shape us. We develop certain frames of references that affect our understanding of and judgments about the world, ourselves, and other people. Many of these judgments limit our functioning and our level of happiness; chronic worriers have allowed them to become a negative part of their internal programming that underscores their life experiences and directs their personal rules for living.

What are your frames of reference? Are they dominated by worry? Take a few moments and answer the following questions:

1. Do you spend a great deal of time thinking about certain areas of your life such as your finances, health, job security, children, family relationships? If so, how much?
2. Does this thinking intrude on other activities and keep you from enjoying yourself?
3. Do you find yourself trying to distract yourself from these thoughts and do the distractions affect your life negatively?
4. Do these thoughts lead you to take specific action to solve the problems or do you spin around the questions?

If you answered "yes" to two or more of these questions, you're stuck in a worry spin cycle and you need to get out.

The answers may be related to a long-standing structure of beliefs that you created years ago when you were a child. We'll explore your architecture of beliefs, and how they play a role in fostering experiences that can make you feel like a victim, in the next chapter. For now, begin to notice how you use these worry filters daily. For example, do you often worry that others don't value you or don't want to be with you? Do you feel self-conscious when you walk into a room of people and have trouble starting conversations? These are the sorts of difficulties that stem from high Beta worry and can have long-term consequences, for example by making you feel like you can never belong to a group.

When you experience more time in Theta and reduce high Beta, you have better access to motivation, creativity, self-control, and better sleep. Continued exposure to a deep state dive in Theta leads to less of the self-criticism, guilt, and shame we often carry over with us from our childhood. When you accomplish the deep dive state four times a week for five to 10 weeks, worry dissolves. The effects are cumulative and the feeling of relaxation lasts long after you complete the exercise. In fact, this amazing state of mind helps you think outside of the rules you have created for yourself to live by. Some are necessary, but some might be dysfunctional. Shake those up, and you can create a breakthrough to the success you deserve in life.

How to Practice Deep State Dive

You will want to follow the script below four days a week and spend 20 minutes at a time in the deepest state. When you find you only worry once in a while, you can continue using the exercise once per week to reinforce its effects.

Notice when you experience your "favorite" worry thoughts and when they occur. As you begin the deep dive experiences, keep track of how worry diminishes over time. Most people like to read the script aloud into a digital recorder or their phone so they can play it back and relax into the deepest mental space possible without having to read instructions. As you follow the exercise and script, you'll notice your mind becoming tranquil and your body following by relaxing deeply. You'll likely see images behind your closed eyes or hear sounds. Try to pay attention to how those images might symbolize a solution that will ease your worry, or what the sounds might be trying to tell you. Your mind will be trying to give you guidance.

Try It Now

Begin with the autogenic exercises—also known as desensitization techniques—below to get you into a self-induced calm and relaxed state of body and mind. Repeat each statement slowly until you begin to feel the effects of the suggestions. Sit upright with your feet flat on the floor in a comfortable and quiet place. You don't want to go to sleep but remain right on the edge of it. Sitting upright will help you maintain the deep state for longer periods of time. Make certain the location where you go into the deep dive is a place where you feel secure and safe.

The Autogenic Exercises

1. My head and face become relaxed and warm.
2. My tongue relaxes and floats in my mouth.
3. My right arm is heavy and warm.
4. My left arm is heavy and warm.
5. My heartbeat is slowing as I relax more and more.
6. My stomach is relaxed and warm.
7. My back is relaxed and warm.
8. My right leg is heavy and warm.
9. My left leg is heavy and warm.
10. My right calf is heavy and warm.
11. My left calf is heavy and warm.
12. My right foot is heavy and warm.
13. My left foot is heavy and warm.
14. I am now completely and deeply relaxed.

Now complete the next phase. Read the script once all the way through before beginning the exercise so you know where you are going. Once you begin recording, pause at least 15 to 30 seconds between each new set of instructions. They might sound unusual, but put your questions and doubts aside; the material is not meant to be cognitively processed, just experienced. So don't think about it too much. Then play the recording back to yourself.

Deep Dive Script

You have to relax all the way to the edge of sleep in order for you to receive information and healing while in the Theta state. To enhance the effect, try doing this exercise near a source of running water. Nature sounds tend to calm the mind quickly, diminishing emotional charges and worry thoughts.

Begin:

1. Find a place to sit and relax without any distractions. Place your feet flat on the floor. Make sure your phone is off and the pets are in another room. If you don't, they will be attracted to the meditative state you produce and want to sit on you, and though it is very sweet of them, a wet tongue on your face can disturb your deep state. Ask your mind for an answer to a question or for

information to guide you on a particular problem that worries you before you begin the relaxation process. Once you ask your mind a question, it will go on an internal search to find the best solution for you. Once you're in a deeply relaxed state, let it go out of your conscious mind.

[Pause 15 to 30 seconds.]

2. Imagine your worry thoughts are like steam rising on a lake in the early morning when the weather is cool. Your worry thoughts move up and out and disappear.

[Pause 15 to 30 seconds.]

3. Adjust your body so you are extremely comfortable. Take a couple of nice deep breaths and begin to allow the sense of comfort it gives you to flow over and through the body. As you sit in your quiet place, just allow the natural calming sensation of the flow of your breath to move from the top of your head to the bottom of your feet.

[Pause 15 to 30 seconds.]

4. Now, slowly, begin to count yourself down from 10 to 1. As each number becomes smaller, feel your relaxation deepening.

10 . . . 9 . . . 8 . . . 7 . . . 6 . . . 5 . . . 4 . . . 3 . . . 2 . . . 1

[Pause 15 to 30 seconds.]

5. Allow yourself to relax even more so you can begin entering a deeper state of mind. Your unconscious is the deepest part of you and a storehouse of everything you learned throughout life. It has amazing abilities to access the most positive resources from within.

[Pause 15 to 30 seconds.]

6. Place your attention on your breathing and imagine you are sinking down to a place where you are twice as relaxed, someplace beneath any sadness, anxiety, depression, or tension and concern. Imagine a blue pool of water. This is your personal pool of self-compassion. You can notice how blue the water is and perhaps you will want to dangle your feet. It's fine if you jump all the way in to feel the soothing quality of the water where love and compassion flows around and into you.

[Pause 15 to 30 seconds.]

7. Now breathe more deeply so that you keep moving down to a place right above sleep. This is your inner sanctuary where

remarkable changes can occur. It is a place of no thought, the deepest mental state possible, and a state of miraculous healing where your brain has the capacity to reset the mind and the body. Allow yourself to float in this space for five to 10 minutes without interruption. If you fall asleep momentarily, it just means you are tired, and gently wake yourself back to the edge of sleep.

As you float you may see dream images arise. If so, allow them to come in without feeling excited. Consider your unconscious mind your oracle, retrieving information and communicating wisdom and advice to you in the form of images, impressions, symbols, or sounds. Ask yourself, "What is my oracle trying to reveal to me?"

[Pause 15 to 30 seconds.]

8. After 10 minutes, begin to give yourself positive suggestions like "The deepest part of my mind knows that I can solve this problem. My mind is powerful and wise. I am more and more confident in my ability to accomplish my goals. Worry leaves my mind like evaporating steam and disappears into the air. A worry thought is a distraction from my best self, so I can let it go. It is a butterfly that for now flits in and out of my head, but I will see it less and less often."

9. Now very gently begin to allow yourself to slowly come back to consciousness as you re-alert. Slowly begin to count up from 1 to 10—1 . . . 2 . . . 3 . . . 4 . . . 5 . . . 6 . . . 7 . . . 8 . . . 9 . . . 10. Gently return your waking attention back into the room. As you count, make an effort to feel your feet, your hands, and your back. Sit quietly for a few minutes. Notice the lighter feeling and sense the internal shift you have made. If your unconscious mind gave you some information, write it down to explore later. If you received interesting images, jot those down. Like any dreams, they will quickly disappear.

10. While you're sitting quietly, consider any information you received in the deep state and how that may help you let go of worry. What other internal resource do you need that will guarantee you behave in the way that allows you to succeed? Is it more confidence, more calm, more knowledge or experience? Now think of someone who has these characteristics. When you are in a stressful situation without knowing exactly what to do, you

could emulate the aspects you admire about a real person or a character in a movie or television show that you want for yourself. We had one client who chose Jethro Gibbs, a character on the TV series *NCIS* who seems to always know the right thing to do in a crisis. In doing so, you'll engage the brain's mirror neurons, those brain cells that respond equally whether you're actually watching or merely imagining someone else perform an action, so you can replicate it. Asking, for example, "What would Gibbs do?" puts you in a resourceful mental state and gives you a moment to think about your reaction and behavior so you can make better choices. Practice imagining what your behavioral model would do in a difficult situation and try copying the mental state and behavior you think he or she would exhibit.

Evelyn Goes for a Dive

We were sure that a deep state dive would help Evelyn calm her mind for longer periods of time than any yoga session or relaxation strategy and get her worry under control.

We helped her descend down to the edge of sleep—the Theta state—and hover there for 20 minutes while going through the script you just read. After a couple of sessions, she began to notice the relaxation she experienced while diving stayed with her for several days, and that her threshold for stressful events increased so she wasn't reacting either as quickly or as violently as before. After 10 sessions of doing the deep state process, she began to notice that her calm state remained with her through the entire week. To her surprise, she began to develop an awareness of her impulses, thoughts, and feelings before she acted on them. It was as though the space between the thought and the consequent action stretched into a moment of reflection that lasted long enough for her to determine whether the behavior would be in her best interest, such as speaking her mind to her boss or staying quiet. She was able to get enough distance to examine how she was interacting with her colleagues and boss and what part she might have played in alienating them as well as inviting her boss's criticism. Once she was able to lower her reactivity and look at her situation at work with clarity, she could set the reactivity aside and consider whether there was another job she might find fulfilling. She began to reprioritize her activities, evaluate what really would be interesting work, and think about how she wanted to contribute to society. She realized that what really interested her was social justice, so she started making specific plans to change her job to one that would allow her to pursue that path. Interestingly, as soon as she made up her mind to start doing what needed to be done (registering for certification classes, perusing the real estate market in case she had to downsize to accommodate her lower salary), she noticed many opportunities coming her way. Her worry, rumination, and resentment dissipated, and she realized that she had all of the internal strength to make the changes she wanted.

Evelyn's time in the deep state of Theta reorganized her thinking. By surrendering to a deep sense of comfort over and over, she was able to access a new sense of self. She found out how empowering it was to be compassionate with herself, and to be able to witness her judgments, worries, fears, and thoughts impartially. She told us they just floated up and out. An added benefit to her newfound awareness was that her taste buds became sensitive to the sugar and chemicals in fast food. As it started to taste bad, she began to lose weight and be attracted to healthier food choices.

She became aware that as a child she had adopted an internal belief that drove her worry and anxious behavior: Like her own mother, whom she frequently heard repeating this mantra, Evelyn often told herself, "I have to worry to make sure things turn out right." Evelyn had watched her mother worry so much she began to believe that it was a necessary condition for solving problems. She thought constantly worrying would ensure she didn't miss anything important and help her avert tragedy. Even though she had left her parents' home long ago, the superstition had followed her and stalled her ability to shift from an agitated mental state to one that was calm and relaxed.

We suggested that Evelyn keep practicing the deep state work a couple of times a week and use the other tools of bilateral stimulation and Mind Wandering to help her calm down when she needed to and continue her personal growth. We also urged her to continue doing deep state work in Theta to gain more control over her thoughts and build immunity to stress.

Another Remarkable Transformation

Don, a middle-aged man, came into the office for help with his second marriage. He was concerned because his wife, Joyce, was communicating with an old boyfriend by email. She swore she had no intention of becoming emotionally involved with her ex, whom she had dated decades before and was also married and living in New Zealand. She had let Don read her emails, and he could see that they were infrequent and brief, and mostly just offered updates on work and family. Don couldn't help feeling skeptical of Joyce's efforts to reassure him; he was really worried he was going to lose her. He knew that he had been overly stressed and emotionally unavailable since enrolling in an MBA program that was taking most of his time, and he feared that even without realizing it, she was seeking companionship.

On top of everything, Don suffered from terrible stress headaches. The more he worried about school and his wife, the worse the headaches became.

We suggested Don might be able to deal with his life better if he could manage the pain and stress first. After 10 deep dive sessions of 20 minutes a session, his headaches disappeared, and his stress was much less intense. (It helps to spend a longer period of time in the deep state if you have headache problems.) Nothing had changed in Don's environment. He was still in a high-pressured graduate program, and his wife was still infrequently interacting with this old friend, but his stress threshold had risen and his emotional reactions were stable.

After the tenth session, Bill asked Don how his marriage was going. Don happily replied that he and his wife had found their way back to each other. In the end, he had realized that his stress was causing him to overreact and the problem was really his own insecurity. As his habitual stress reactions disappeared, he had greater clarity and insight, and he was no longer mistaking a rock (the boyfriend) for a lion (a threat). He took up meditation. A few years later, Bill ran into Don. Don still was headache free, and he and his wife were closer than ever.

Power Thought: *You can dissolve worry and find peace and comfort by resting in the deepest mental state before sleep for five to 10 minutes.*

––––––––––

Now you have a better understanding of an ancient yet modern brain-change tool that melts worry. The next step is to look at the underlying ideas you carry around that promote worry. In Chapter 5 we will examine the architecture of your belief system, how it limits you, and how to use future-oriented visualizations and questions to guide your actions to create the best day and life possible.

CHAPTER 5

Future Think
to Regain Your
Optimism

Worry never robs tomorrow of its sorrow,
it only saps today of its joy.

—Leo F. Buscaglia

How we think determines how we live. When we perceive the world through an optimistic lens and approach new circumstances and situations without fear or cynicism, we tend to be pretty satisfied with our life. Things are never perfect, of course, yet all but the most catastrophic incidents generally seem manageable. But when we take a pessimistic view of the world and approach it with fear, fretting over all the negative things that could happen, negative things often seem to follow. It's a bit of a self-fulfilling prophecy. Of course, there are those who will say that worrying over what could happen is pragmatic, not pessimistic. Preparing for the worst and being pleasantly surprised when it doesn't happen are a lot better than being thrown totally off guard when things go wrong, isn't it? No, it really isn't, because all that time and energy and brain space you're using to worry is time and energy and brain space you could be using to chart a brighter future. This chapter will help you redirect your thinking to stimulate the brain's GPS for the future by using visualization, future-oriented questions, and an action plan that ensures you take a positive focus.

When we visualize a negative future, we stimulate high Beta brain waves and increase our worry. While reviewing your worst-case scenarios is the brain's way of keeping you safe, when done too often it also serves to condition the worry habit. Future Thinking, on the other hand, stimulates Alpha waves and dopamine, which renders your mind worry-free. Unlike Mind Wandering, where you let your mind visit places and scenarios from your past that make you relaxed and happy, Future Thinking asks you to actively imagine scenarios that you want to see happen. By deliberately considering the best possible future, you put in place a process that propels you in that direction. Future Thinking also builds intention and motivation, which allows you to more easily achieve goals and overcome difficulties.

Consider Marina. She was facing the biggest challenge in her life: In just a few weeks, she would move to Paris to pursue a wonderful career opportunity as an IT project manager. But she was intensely worried. She had a boyfriend and she was close to her parents, and she couldn't stop ruminating on how her move could affect her relationships. She had also never lived outside her native Houston, much less the country, and she was scared of what could happen in a city that had recently weathered terrible terrorist attacks and seemed to be struggling with political unrest. She thought about backing out, but she couldn't bear to lose such a great opportunity to advance her IT career and learn new skills, especially in such a lovely place. On one hand, she'd get excited envisioning herself walking along the Seine, enjoying evenings at the bistro speaking French with new friends, visiting museums and immersing herself in French culture. On the other hand, she imagined her terror should she find herself sitting at a bistro or riding the metro if someone walked in with a bomb. Her imagination was so strong she could send herself into a panic imagining the chaos and fear. In addition, she was afraid of not doing well on the job. The internal conflict she felt between following a path toward something she wanted to do and avoiding her worst fear was almost physically painful. Her chest frequently ached and she had a constant headache. Her dark fears began to cast deep shadows on all aspects of her life, including her relationship with her steady boyfriend and parents. Though she knew her days to enjoy their company were waning, she found herself snapping at the people most precious to her, and she was unable to sleep at night.

Marina decided to make an appointment with her primary physician, who diagnosed her with an anxiety disorder and prescribed anti-anxiety medication plus an antidepressant. The medicines made her feel dissociated, nauseated, and shaky. Her physician reassured her that if the symptoms didn't lessen in three weeks, he'd prescribe another drug to counteract the side effects. Her body finally adjusted, but she noticed a peculiar numbness, as though her emotions and feelings were being smothered in a feather comforter. Her thoughts seemed to come more slowly, too.

Eager to find an alternative to pills, Marina sought us out. We acknowledged her emotional pain, but assured her that her brain could be her ally as she prepared for a prolonged separation from the people she loved. All she had to do was retrain it to help her see the future in a positive light instead of a fearful one.

Marina's fears of living in a city plagued by violence were not unfounded. The October 2015 terrorist attacks had occurred only months earlier, and the group responsible for it had struck again in Belgium, only because investigators thwarted their next attack on France. However, ruminating about potential danger could actually put her in more danger. If she perceived everything as equally dangerous, she wouldn't notice if her intuition ever told her that something in particular looked unsafe. We needed to give her brain a chance to recalibrate so that it could alert her to danger without obsessing over everything that could go wrong.

To begin, we had her list the facts, as she knew them, about the possibility versus the probability of danger. She took a piece of paper and listed:

1. Paris has been attacked twice and most of the perpetrators have been caught or killed.
2. The city remains on alert and has increased security.
3. My place of business has excellent security, as does the area where I will live.

As she reviewed her list, Marina was comforted by the realization that her chances of being hurt were small.

Intention

Ruminating on things that may or may not happen is wearisome; fixating on a goal is empowering. The brain is uniquely built for setting an intention in place. For example, have you ever noticed that once you have decided to buy a particular car model, you start to see that car everywhere? It's like your brain is trying to reassure you that you made a good choice by revealing all the other car owners who made it, too. Once you set an intention, your mind works the same way to support your decision. Marina decided she would relocate to Paris, and once she did, she became open to experiences that would reinforce the goal. For example, she met a colleague who had just returned from working in Paris and had nothing but wonderful things to say about the experience. Because her colleague had first-hand information about the safety precautions Paris was taking, this serendipitous meeting helped Marina think more positively about relocating to that beautiful city, which meant she approached her adventure in a positive frame of mind, which meant she left herself more open to experiences that would support her positive outlook than those that might dampen her enthusiasm. Positive thinking causes a snowball effect of positive events.

Motivation and Enthusiasm

The next step would be to activate Marina's motivation and enthusiasm, which encourage our brains to produce a combination of

Alpha and low Beta, which increases laser-like attention and consequently decreases worry. Neurobiologist Dr. Gerald Huther suggests that when we are excited or emotionally moved by something, our brain releases neuroplastic chemicals to help us harness the intense feeling of enthusiasm that allows us to solve problems, win a game of tennis, or create something amazing.[1]

Negative Mental Rehearsal

To help Marina feel more secure and courageous, it was important to track down the moment when her excitement about her upcoming adventure turned to fear. She wasn't really sure, but as we talked she mentioned that upon hearing her big announcement her mother blurted, "Enjoy your time with us before you take that new job! You never know if you're coming back." There it was! Her mother's powerful suggestion had pierced her mind and stuck there like an invisible thorn that dug in deeper every time she envisioned the future.

It is not uncommon for a seemingly minor comment to have such a huge impact on a person. In fact, in tribal cultures, woe to you if your shaman decided to "point the bone" at you. The bone sometimes had a point at the end and the shaman would sing a curse of illness or death over it. Often, the person who wound up the target of the bone's powerful voodoo would collapse. His blood pressure would drop, his heart would flutter, and death would occur in a short while. Why? Was the bone really cursed? Of course not, but our cultural expectations are formidable, and the person on the receiving end of the bone had probably been trained from a young age to believe that it *was* cursed. When someone close to us or in authority makes a negative declaration that rings with the power of "truth," it can have a major influence on our imagination and make us hugely susceptible to a parasympathetic shutdown—a complete collapse of the body's nervous system that can lower blood pressure and heart rate to such an extent that a person may faint and even die. The opposite is true as well; the shaman could deliver a healing spell or administer an herbal concoction that may have been utterly useless, yet have similarly powerful effects as his negative incantation due to his patient's belief in the concoction's efficacy.

Marina's mother unintentionally acted like an ancient shaman pronouncing a curse.

Trying to be helpful, Marina's physician may have unintentionally done the same thing.

By telling her she had an anxiety disorder and needed strong medication, he implied that she had no control over herself, and that negative states just happen and nothing but medication can alter them.

Sometimes when we think we're alerting someone to danger or being "realistic," we're actually inadvertently creating a negative suggestion in that person's mind, or offering him or her a nocebo—a negative suggestion. Here's how you know the difference: The more there is a 1:1 correlation between a person's actions and negative consequences, such as texting while driving, or eating junk, or playing with fire, the more important it is to alert that person to the potential negative consequences. But when situations do not correlate 1:1, telling someone emphatically that he or she is going to suffer a negative outcome puts the idea of that negative outcome in the person's mind. It encourages people to look at their situation through a negative lens, and as we established earlier, negative thinking can create a self-fulfilling prophecy. Our mind hears that negative pronouncement and, feeling protective, starts rehearsing a negative future, which then can lead us closer to behaviors that actually make that negative future come to pass. Of course physicians in particular are always walking a fine line. A patient with high blood pressure and high blood sugar might be a heart attack waiting to happen. A doctor would be derelict if she didn't provide medical assistance and encourage her patient to make lifestyle changes. How the patient interprets that advice, however, is often all about the tone and language in which the advice is delivered. If he hears criticism and threats, he's going to feel overwhelmed and helpless and his brain is likely to urge him to retreat into defensiveness and denial. If he hears encouragement and especially the message that he has control over the outcome of this situation, he's much more likely to feel empowered, motivated, and enthusiastic about making changes in his life, which, with the right support, can become reality. The same thing goes for mental health doctors. We do our patients a disservice when we automatically reach for the prescription pad without explaining to our patients that the drugs are often there to support their own efforts, and that they have the power to help themselves. Language is powerful, especially when it comes from the mouths of health-care professionals. It's something we all need to be aware of.

Indeed, the newest science indicates that many elements play a role in how or whether people develop mental problems. Besides the well-known culprits such as poor nutrition and sleep, the causes can also be our own negative internal states and thinking patterns, a dearth of fun and laughter, and a lack of education in how to turn down fear.

Kelly Brogan, physician and author of *A Mind of Your Own*, reports from her medical research that there are three main resolvable triggers that contribute to the kind of worry that can lead to depression. The first is inflammation, which can be caused by stress, a diet high in simple carbohydrates and sugars, insufficient exercise, or a microbial imbalance. The second is prescription drugs and their side effects, such as a fuzzy mind. The third influence may be the pathologizing of emotion by physicians and psychologists.[2]

Although the short-term use of some medications can be useful, without offering brain training to develop new mind habits, doctors are only addressing the symptoms of a worried mind, not the habitual mental states that cause the problems. And though they often make people feel better for the short term, psychotropic cocktails can eventually make patients feel worse.

Robert Whitaker, researcher and author of *Anatomy of an Epidemic*, wrote a chilling account of how the country's drug-based care paradigm fuels an epidemic of mental disorders and ultimately makes symptoms such as worry and rumination worse.[3] He asked: Are we running the risk of turning worry-ridden people into mental patients? For example, the use of benzodiazepines often rebounds to increase a patient's worry and anxiety and can finally lead to depression. Getting off of this class of drugs is incredibly difficult. For some people, psychotherapy is equally effective for ridding them of worry as antidepressants, and the withdrawal, is a whole lot easier.

In fact, the newest research on anti-anxiety medications and antidepressants finds that 80 percent of the reduction in symptoms is due to a placebo effect.[4] Just as negative suggestions or nocebos can influence us mentally and physically in dramatic ways and create a negative future orientation, placebos can inspire physical changes while creating a positive future orientation. Someone who responds positively to a placebo isn't lying to himself; he really does feel better because the placebo prompted him to enter a mental state that allowed him to envision a positive future. Scientists don't yet understand exactly how, but studies have shown over and over again that positive Future Thinking and visualization can literally trigger a healing response in the body, affecting chemistry, muscular changes, and gene expression. That's not to say we shouldn't accept medications; they can offer great relief and a supportive boost to our own healing efforts. But it's important to respect the body's amazing capacity for healing and restoring balance. It can become difficult to sort out how much of your healing is due to your own mind's capacity versus the pill you popped into your mouth.

Your mind is more powerful than you know. If you want to change your life or even your health, often the first place to start is to change where you focus your attention. That was our next step with Marina.

We armed her with a tool that would help her direct her brain toward the most positive future she could imagine, even while still feeling fearful. The tool? Questions. Future-oriented questions, to be exact. Good questions are empowering. Bad questions create more pain. Because of the brain's negative bias, most of the time the questions we ask ourselves are asked in the negative: "Why can't I accomplish this goal?" "Why do I have to go through this?" They're legitimate questions, but too often they position you as a victim. Sticking to a "Why me?" line of questions stimulates more negative thinking. Worry questions can never be answered in a satisfying way. Negative questions lay down a neural pathway that makes you an expert in negative thinking. Put simply, your brain does what you ask it to do.

Marina was plagued by a neverending loop of negative thoughts about the future. She thought that by paying attention to them, she'd be able to control them, but instead her focus on them simply created more worry. We suggested that Marina stop analyzing the negative "Why me?" thoughts and try shifting her attention toward solutions by answering these future-oriented questions:

- What do I need in order to feel safe and secure going to Paris?
- What do I need to do to be successful at the new job?
- How can I feel better without medication?

Once she knew the answers to those questions, she could come up with solutions, such as video chats to help her cope with the separation from her loved ones, planning to book a visit home to the States every now and then, and inviting her family to visit her. Marina would smile as she daydreamed how much fun it would be to meander through the streets of the City of Light with her boyfriend.

Every time Marina started worrying, she'd interrupt her negative train of thought with a mantra: "I am capable. I am strong. I can keep myself safe." She learned to keep a vision of a positive future in her mind, and it actually came true. She traveled to Paris and was immediately charmed by the beautiful city. Being there in person allowed her to witness all that was being done to protect the city from terrorists. By the time her boyfriend came to visit her three months later, she was ready to ask if he'd consider moving there with her so she could pursue a long-term position in the French office.

Future Orientation in Time

The next step in successful problem resolution is to use a powerful mental time travel visualization to imagine how the future will look once your goal has been achieved, and then become aware of the steps it would take to get there.

In the clinical hypnosis literature, Future Orientation in Time is sometimes called "pseudo orientation in time." In this technique, you visualize yourself at a time in the future when you have successfully solved the problem that is currently bothering you. Imagine how you would look, sound, dress, and behave at that time. Then imagine stepping into that future person, seeing through her eyes, hearing through her ears, and thinking as she would. Your successful future self becomes a resource for instruction on how to accomplish the steps you need to take to that future success. List these steps and think about how to implement them. This future focus increases intention, motivation, and enthusiasm.

The process looks like this:

1. Activate your motivation to move toward a specific future with a morning ritual of reading something uplifting and specifically related to your goal. By reaching for inspiration, you access positive expectations and enthusiasm about the future. Write down what your specific future will do for you. By writing down your goal, you mentally rehearse the goal. Continue doing this over time. Feel the excitement of motivation and notice your enthusiasm when you contemplate a future where you have successfully achieved the goal. It is impossible to experience enthusiasm and worry at the same time.

2. Next, create an intention to do what it takes to accomplish your goal and visualize yourself taking the first step toward that future.

3. Trigger your persistence by committing to the process. You will probably grow bored with a long-term endeavor at some point, so think about how you will stretch through that feeling to the other side. Draft the rest of your plan in three to five steps to get from where you are now to the future you want. Include benchmarks and deadlines to keep yourself on track. Write down the potential obstacles to completing these steps. Answer the question: What has to happen to ensure you follow through with these steps?

4. Use mental rehearsal to explore the future you want. Don't complain about what you don't have or what you've failed to do. Instead, visualize every day having accomplished the end goal and hold some symbol of

the goal in mind. If the goal is writing a book, imagine holding the book; if the goal is increasing your client load, imagine the inquiries or commissions coming in.

5. Go back and record the fulfillment dates of each action step as you complete it.

The Power of Delayed Gratification

You will improve your chances of achieving any goal if you increase your ability to delay gratification. You've likely heard of the famous marshmallow experiment conducted by Walter Mischel and his team at Stanford University in the late 1960s and early 1970s. Scientists sat a series of volunteer children between 4 and 5 years of age at a table. They placed a marshmallow in front of each child with instructions that he or she could eat the marshmallow right away. However, they added, if the child could wait 15 minutes while the researchers completed an errand, the youngster could have two marshmallows. Many of the children quickly ate the one marshmallow. Others tried to resist the temptation, but it grew harder and harder as they sat looking at it. The researchers later gave these children mental strategies to take their minds off their inner conflict, such as instructing them to imagine there was a picture frame around the marshmallow that made it look like a photograph instead of the real deal. The kid who used visualization to boost their resolve showed a greater ability to wait longer for the second marshmallow than kids who did not. The study showed that self-control could be learned.

In follow-up studies through the children's lives, the people who delayed gratification or who trained their brains to be more disciplined had higher SAT scores, lower levels of substance abuse, lower likelihood of obesity, better responses to stress, better social skills, and generally handled life without much worry and struggle. Brain scans revealed these subjects had more activity in the part of the brain responsible for problem-solving. Those subjects who could wait managed their reactions better—and worried little. By training their brains to be more disciplined, they became more successful adults.

Try It Now

Think about an issue that worries you. Make it into a still picture and place a mental frame around it. Minimize the picture on your mental screen and move it to the lower right corner of your visual field. Notice how the worry dissipates. By making the image smaller, you dissociate from the charge of the issue.

The contents of your mind itself stimulate brain states. Let's say you're focusing on not having enough money. You might respond with worry and avoidance, and then try making yourself feel better by moving money around from one account to another or by trying to make more money. If you become over aroused in a fight-flight-freeze scenario, however, you might blame your situation on others, or impulsively decide to sell your car, or go to a loan shark where you'll get more in debt. You might freeze and avoid thinking about the situation, allowing the worry to fester in the back of your mind. Or you could calm yourself down by using any of the tools we have discussed and find an appropriate solution. Brain states access and transform mental content. The children who demonstrated self-control incorporated a rule for living, namely that self-control gives you more freedom because you choose solutions that are more functional.

Limiting Beliefs

Unfortunately, even people with the greatest self-control likely have a "limiting belief," a belief about how the world works that can curtail their freedom, interfere with their confidence, persistence, and motivation, keep them in chronic worry, and hold them back from their greatest potential. These beliefs are usually unconscious, but they can impede your life unless you identify them and dissolve them. To be the best version of yourself most of the time, it is important to become aware of any limiting belief that interferes with your ideal self. How do you become consciously aware of that which is unconscious? Clues to these old ideas may come in the form of personal rules for living. For example, one rule you hold dear might be that you should never be late. Though it is useful to leave early and try to imagine things that could delay you like road construction, inevitably, you will sometimes encounter unforeseen obstacles that will occasionally make you late. It is important to realize there will be exceptions to your rules so that when they occur you don't experience frantic worry and make up consequences that are unlikely to occur.

Belief Architecture

When you were younger than 6 years old, your unconscious mind absorbed family rules and models for living in the form of gestures, tones of voice, sounds of laughter and anger, and how Mom and Dad looked at and spoke to each other. The essentials that hold the family together—their values, ethics, methods for working out conflict, expressions of love and affection, trust and honesty—became part of your awareness. By the time you were a little older, between the ages of 6 and 13, you began to learn about the world beyond your family. Your family's rules and perceptions and your understanding of these rules and perceptions determined how cheerful you were and your relationship to food, men, women, pets, work, and your own spirituality. You were highly influenced by all of these elements, and together they formed your architecture of beliefs. This scaffolding influences every decision you make and perception you construct, and is highly influential in whether you develop and activate worry.

Our limiting beliefs reveal themselves in a number of ways if we know where to look. Often they cause feelings of fear, worry, impatience, or frustration. They are often the source of our inner critic. If you write down your inner critic's comments you'll often realize that you've been carrying them around with you for a very long time, most likely since childhood.

One of the three pillars holding up the architecture of your limiting beliefs is your biological wiring. Children demonstrate early on a tendency toward extroversion or introversion. Extroverts recharge their batteries by being with other people. Introverts recharge by being alone. An extrovert's limiting belief may be that it is not okay to be alone and be somewhat uncomfortable. An introvert could have the opposite limiting belief that it is too difficult to be with others to accomplish a goal.

The next pillar is your mindset, or your psychology. As we've established, how positive or negative you are and what you believe about yourself and the world shapes how events affect your life and can even influence what actually happens to you.

The third pillar in your architecture of beliefs is your default internal state and accompanying trains of emotions, thoughts, attitudes, and behaviors. Believing in your ability to accomplish what you set your mind to is a huge driver toward success and lets you develop your horizon opening beliefs. Your internal state of confidence, certainty, and happiness promotes you forward to take risks.

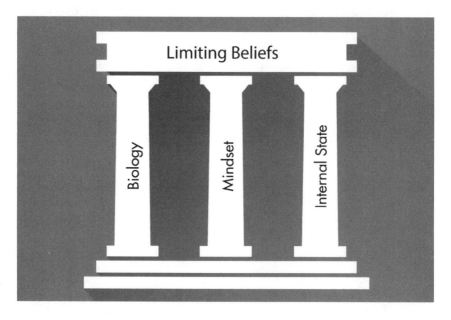

Let's say you realize that throughout your entire childhood you were told, "You can't get what you want." But if you practice Future Thinking and make sure you do those things that make you joyful, enthusiastic, and persistent, you'll see very soon that that's just not true, because the process will let you see how you can accomplish any goal with enough data, time, support, and resources. In order to live an extraordinary life, you may need to construct a new model of reality. The next story illustrates how one young man rejected the limited mindset someone tried to impose over him by upholding the pillars of a positive attitude, courage, and persistence.

The Brain's Visualization Superpowers

The son of an itinerant horse trainer loved to help his father. Work was hard to come by but training the horses was fulfilling. The boy and his father had to be flexible to make an income, so they were frequently required to relocate to different cities. During the boy's senior year of high school, he was asked to write a paper about what he wanted to become in the future. The young man wrote several pages. He wanted to own a 200-acre horse ranch, have a 4,000-square-foot ranch home, and all of the other buildings including the barn and horse track. He designed the ranch on paper and turned it in with the essay to the teacher. Two days later, he received the paper back with an F and a note that said, "See me after class." When the boy asked what was wrong with the paper, the teacher replied that his dream was impossible; he came from such humble beginnings that he would never accomplish such a grand dream. If he wanted to rewrite the paper and focus on an achievable goal, the teacher would consider revising the grade. The young man was devastated and asked his father what he should do. The father said it was his son's decision, but emphasized that it was a very important one that would definitely affect his future. The boy pondered a long time. He went back to school and told the teacher, "You keep your grade, and I will keep my dream." The boy was Monty Roberts, who became an internationally successful "horse whisperer" and bestselling author. He built his 200-acre horse ranch, too.[5]

Monty Roberts challenged the authority and the limiting beliefs of his teacher by maintaining his confidence that he could create the future of his dreams.

Challenge Your Beliefs

When you have doubts or worries about the future, make a list of the things you think you can't accomplish or what you're afraid to try, and ask yourself what adventures you've kept yourself from having because of each of them. How many did you miss because of real obstacles, and how many because of unsubstantiated, self-imposed beliefs?

Now do this exercise:

1. Write the new belief you want to practice. Doing this will begin to upgrade your inner mental software.
2. Visualize the new future where these beliefs will carry you, such as "I can accomplish what I set my mind to," or "All I need to reach my goal are several action steps and new data."
3. Imagine blood flowing to your hands and feet by thinking about sitting in front of a fireplace. Repeat the following: warm hands, warm feet, warm heart. Do this until you can sense a change in your body temperature.
4. Focus on changing your physiology to change your brain state to Alpha. Breathing more deeply or focusing on a pleasant scene will produce Alpha. You might take two to three nice deep breaths. Allow any tension in the body to relax. Ask yourself: What are my priorities and what do I want to do? Is my goal really worthy of me? Am I willing to pay the price to accomplish this goal? What are the costs versus the rewards? Keep in mind that there are no right or wrong answers, and that there is risk in everything. The bottom line is, you want to pursue whatever it is you imagine that lights up your life. You can always change your mind later.
5. Now repeat these statements: I am calm and relaxed. I can imagine the future I desire without worry. I am moving in the direction of my most preferred future.
6. Imagine that anyone who has been unsupportive moves up and out of your mind and leaves the room. Now give yourself a hug while imagining your future self giving you a hug and telling you that what you can imagine, you can master.

Now that you have explored Future Thinking and ridding yourself of limiting beliefs, let's take the final steps in putting worry at bay and creating the life you want.

Try It Now

Create your perfect life. You are not allowed to factor in any of the challenges or obstacles that might stand between you and what you want. Answer the following questions abiding by one simple rule: *No worries*.

Create Your Perfect Day

1.   Where would you wake up?
2.   Who would you wake up with?
3.   What breakfast would you eat?
4.   What would you do in the morning?
5.   What lunch would you eat?
6.   Who would you have lunch with?
7.   What would you do in the afternoon?
8.   Who would you be with?
9.   Where in the world would you be?
10. Who would you see in the afternoon or would you prefer to be alone?
11. Where would you go for dinner and with whom would you be?
12. How would you spend your evening and where would you go?
13. How would you end your day?
14. Where would you go to bed and whom would you be with?

The answers to these questions highlight what you value and pinpoint areas that may be out of balance in your life. As you answer these questions, rather than worrying about them, let the future you desire to create be your guide.

Your Best Month

Write down what you want to accomplish in a month. You might want to include that you're going to worry less now that you have several worry-removing tools at your disposal. Fully consider what a really great month would look like. Write down even those things you aren't sure you can accomplish.

Your Dream Year

What do you want to accomplish this year and what needs to happen for you to have a dream year? Where do you want to go, whom do you want to go with, and are these business adventures or personal ones? Break it down into categories:

1. Personal.
2. Family.
3. Health and fitness.
4. Adventures.

We have discussed how the power of visualization and asking future-oriented questions can set your inner GPS. These are tools you can use every day to navigate toward your best future. When you use them intentionally, you shut down the worry mind, create enthusiasm and excitement, and gain certainty that you have the ability to accomplish your most cherished goals. Now instead of trying to do damage control against things that haven't happened yet, you have a clear vision of what you want and a personal plan of action to get you there.

Power Thought: *When you replace worry with positive expectation, you have the clarity to envision, plan, and execute your best possible future.*

––––––

The next chapter will show you how to turn on and off certain emotional circuits at will and with practice, develop your own inner remote control device to stay on the right emotional channel.

PART III

Train Your State

CHAPTER 6

Change Your Emotional Channels

If you treat every situation as a life and
death matter, you'll die a lot of times.

—Dean Smith

Gabriella's teenage son is driving her car—and driving her crazy. She can't sleep until she hears his keys in the door at night because she's sure he's going to get in a wreck, and who knows whom he's got in that car with him, and she hopes it isn't that Raymond kid because she can tell just by looking at him that he smokes weed.

To make matters worse, college expenses are looming, and she's scared that she's not going to have enough to cover it all and if she can she'll probably never take another vacation as long as she lives and damn her ex for giving a dime to that other woman's kids. She's tried to solve the problem by taking on additional freelance clients, but one of them is an incredible pill to work with, and when she tried to tell her mom about it last week, Gabriella saw this vacant look that made her wonder if Mom is getting Alzheimer's, and if she is, forget getting any help from her siblings. Gabriella just knows it'll all be on her.

Sound familiar? Is there a similar Stephen King–worthy horror show of worries flipping through your mind? If so, there's a way you can hit the pause button on that awful mental movie and recondition your brain to see the world in much less fearful terms.

Gabriella's situation was understandably scary and overwhelming. But we knew that if we could help her shift her focus of attention, she could calm her mind and problem-solve without harming herself in the process. Then she could learn how to shift out of scary and worrisome thinking, learn how to change a dead-end life pattern, and condition her brain to run smoothly.

We introduced Gabriella to neuro-repatterning, a tool that could revolutionize her quality of life. Why neuro-repatterning? It's a powerful and effective strategy that reconditions your mind and regulates the stimulation of your emotional circuits. By becoming aware of which circumstances activate which emotional circuits, you give yourself more of a choice in how you act on these feelings and how to activate opposing circuits, which gives you the freedom to understand and respond to others more appropriately.

Through neuro-repatterning you can develop more control over your emotions, dissolve worry, transform negative ideas, and balance the intensity of your internal states. You simply need to figure out what events or thoughts trigger your worry and retrain your brain to react less intensely to those thoughts and events by turning on a different circuit. With practice, neuro-repatterning works at a deep level to improve your focus and pinpoint your optimal zone for happiness and productivity. Your reality is malleable when you learn what to do. This is also a tool that will ultimately help you get ready to move into optimal states of consciousness.

We've already established that our limiting beliefs are generally formed by our childhood experiences and supported by the three pillars of the architecture of belief—our biology, our mindset, and our default internal state. Limiting beliefs are not only problematic because they often keep us from attempting to achieve goals, however, but also because over time they create negative life patterns that spread into broader areas of life. One of Gabriella's limiting beliefs was that she was the only person who would properly take care of her mother. As a result, she not only worried about her mother, but also never asked her siblings to take on some responsibility or confronted them about pitching in their fair share of the work. She was uncomfortable sticking up for herself and reluctant to engage in confrontation with difficult people. Another of her limiting beliefs was that she would never have enough money. Consequently, she also had a life pattern of over-functioning from thinking she was responsible for everything and everyone, and it drained her energy to do other things.

Let's look at how Gabriella developed her limiting beliefs and life patterns. Gabriella grew up in a household where there was never enough money to go around. She was the oldest child whose parents put her in charge of her younger brother and sister. Her parents had to work a lot to make ends meet, so she took the role of a third parent. Of course, she often couldn't get her siblings to mind her. Her parents did the best they could on a limited income but criticized her for not getting her siblings to behave when she was left alone with them. Gabriella always felt under pressure to take care of more things around the house than she could. When her father died, her responsibilities intensified, and Gabriella had to juggle caretaking and cooking for her siblings. Unable to develop her own social network and often alone, she came to the conclusion that everything was up to her. Afraid to rock the boat through any adolescent adventure, she developed a cautious life pattern. She was a model teenager, following the rules to a tee without indulging in any of the typical adolescent adventures or experimentations. And all the while, deprived of the virtual oxygen of friends, spontaneity, whimsical thinking, and big dreams, her life energy was shutting down.

Gabriella's isolation continued into adulthood. Though her siblings were functional grownups, as kids they had never been taken to task when they didn't do their share of the chores around the house. They continued this pattern by not helping out with their mother.

Gabriella felt unappreciated at work, too. She had a good job, she was underpaid for her level of expertise. But rather than asking her employer for more compensation, she would take freelance work to supplement her income. The additional money helped, but the extra work hours were exhausting. Meanwhile, her husband brought in an income but left her to do most of the child rearing, preferring to be the "fun" parent when he spent time with the kids. Gabriella's resentment grew. Eventually he left and they divorced. Ironically, he married a woman who expected him to be a full-time father to her children both financially and emotionally.

Gabriella came by her predicaments honestly. Her life experiences had led to limiting beliefs that had morphed into life patterns that left her overburdened, unable to set boundaries, and incapable of getting her needs met. Worry was her constant companion. Her life energy—a force called *chi* in some cultures, or *élan vital* in French, and crucial to enjoying life—was depleted.[1] She was numb, dissociated, and disconnected. She was an overworked, underpaid, exhausted single mom and still her mother's primary caretaker. Something had to give.

How the Past Affects the Present

Every thought and mental state you experience creates chemical reactions. When you are negative you flood your organs with norepinephrine or adrenaline; when you feel joyful and grateful you activate the feel-good chemicals called endorphins. When you enter your habitual mental states, you develop a routine practice of being and feeling a certain way. What are yours? How positive are they? If you have been angry with someone for years, you have conditioned your internal state and your body's responses to staying in resentment or disappointment. What do you need to do to let go of the past? The more you ruminate about what happened, the more you live there and not in the present. When you think about a past event that still carries an emotional charge (whether it's a good thing like winning your school spelling bee or a bad thing like getting dumped), your brain re-creates the same pattern as when the event occurred, reinforcing the exact pattern of neuronal firing and wiring. Worrying about the past keeps the past showing up at your front door. As you keep repeating the same emotional state, you train yourself to fire the same automatic pattern. Eventually you develop a habit that makes it very hard to see that life is giving you brand-new experiences that don't necessitate the same kind of behaviors and emotional states. By reacting inappropriately to these new stimuli and experiences you can force the present to start replicating the past. When you live in the past, it is difficult to have or appreciate new experiences. And yet we need new experiences if we are to grow.

What Do We Really Need?

The experiences and relationships of our youth tend to influence the circuitry of our emotions, forming the neural foundation of our inner lives and shaping our capacity to regulate our feelings. Early attachment conditioning establishes the neural patterning of emotional systems that remains in place across a lifetime.[2] When caregivers respond appropriately to children's feelings by soothing negative states and encouraging positive ones, children learn how to calm themselves and develop secure attachments. Adults with secure attachments have the ability to be both intimate and connected and be independent and separate. Developmental researcher Allan Schore demonstrated that the brains of children with secure attachments develop differently from insecurely attached children. People with insecure attachments feel overly worried about the separation when they need to be apart from a partner and may cling to relationships. Or they may feel so worried and hurt when experiencing separation they will ignore the partner as a way of protecting themselves against anxious feelings.[3]

Caregivers influence the attachment styles of children through their psychobiological attunement. The way they gaze at children, their nurturing sounds, the frequency of their touch, the stability of their moods—all of these affect whether and to what degree children are able to make healthy emotional connections.Connecting is just one of several primal human needs. Fortunately, we can build connections as adults even if we don't develop them in childhood. Neuroplasticity—the ability of the brain to adapt by building new neural pathways—means we can use mental training to establish a sense of internal security and fulfill our unmet needs.

Human needs are the innate psychological essentials for living. They include the need for security and order, the need for novelty, the need for growth, contribution, status, and the need for feeling connected to a community. When any of these are out of balance, we feel out of sorts and worry that something is missing in life. As we have established, unmet needs also tend to signal negative life patterns.

Whether your needs are met or not will affect your brain's EEG. When you feel hopeless you may have high Delta frequency, which makes your mind fuzzy. If you learned a life pattern of insecurity as a child, your Beta may be turned on high in sympathetic arousal, making it difficult to calm down. At times you may find yourself bored with work and feel a need to grow in a different area. Your Theta frequency may rise as you emotionally check out. Delta may rise if you are not connected to a community and contributing your time and expertise. Feeling like you matter is important, and feeling unimportant may lead to high Theta and being dissociated in a parasympathetic downward spiral, which can turn into depression. The times you feel in the flow of life, it is likely your needs are being fulfilled and your EEG is in balance; when your needs are not met, it is more difficult to shift your internal states and pull out of self-destructive moods and mindsets.

Human needs attach to seven different emotional circuits, each coded with their unique language. They are Seeking or Curiosity, Rage, Fear, Lust, Care or Nurturing, Panic, and Play. [4] These emotional patterns are often triggered by familiar phrases we heard frequently in our youth, and once activated can immediately shift our thinking and motivation patterns. For example, depending on the voice inflection, the question "What's that?" can trigger fear or curiosity. In addition, these automatic processes can unconsciously direct lifelong behaviors and relationship dynamics. If you know how to coach your brain circuits to work for you, however, you can shut down worry.

Let's look at these emotional circuits up close:

1. **Seeking/Curiosities:** When this circuit is activated, you experience curiosity, novelty, anticipation, excitement, intentionality, and a directed purpose. You also seek accomplishments and rewards. Children are constantly activating this circuit because they naturally love to explore their environments. Adults trigger it when they open to explore new ideas, places, events, and interests. Seeking can also activate cravings and addictions, because it releases dopamine, which gives us a wonderful feeling that we often want to keep having. Someone who has a balanced Seeking circuit will be dedicated to an endeavor; someone who is out of balance is frequently bored and compulsively sets new goals. When this system is underactive due to psychological pain, depression sets in. This circuit needs stimulation to activate an interest in living. It also contributes to the flow state, a peak performance state of mind that we'll explore in detail in Chapter 9. Because this circuit helps you explore the world, you can call it your Pioneer.

   Need: Curiosity and novelty.

   Positive Life Pattern: "I have the desire to learn new things, be open to new experiences, new relationships, and adventures."

   Negative Life Pattern: "As soon as I achieve something, I must go on to the next level." "I need more novelty to feel satisfied." "I need substances, food, or things to feel good about myself or my life."

2. **Rage:** This circuit activates feelings of frustration, thoughts of blame and contempt, memories of being hurt and having been misunderstood and maligned, and the impulse to attack an offender. It promotes

self-protection in dangerous situations. Rage immediately shuts off the Seeking Circuit, which is why we can lose perspective and experience tunnel vision in this state. You could call this system your Protector.

Need: Well-being, security, and justice.

Positive Life Pattern: To protect; defend; overcome fear; place yourself in harm's way to protect others; take necessary actions you wouldn't normally choose to take, such as in war.

Negative Life Pattern: Rage can cause us to become unfocused and do more damage than is necessary to protect ourselves or others. Unfocused rage can lead to being less effective. "No one tells me what to do" or "I must retaliate."

3. **Fear:** A circuit that activates the flight, fight, or freeze responses, as well as worry and rumination. Under threat, it activates to mobilize or immobilize a person in the presence of a dangerous person or event. You could call this circuit your Safety Manager.

   Need: Safety and security.

   Positive Life Pattern: "I pay attention to potential danger or threats."

   Negative Life Pattern: "I will be easily harmed or judged."

4. **Lust:** This circuit stimulates movement toward intimacy and sexual expression. It turns on in response to visual and verbal cues, or hormonal fluctuations and physical touch. You could call this system your Lover.

   Need: To experience sexual release and physical touch, which is best experienced in a bonded relationship.

   Positive Life Pattern: "I can connect sexually and be interested enough to please a partner and accept being pleased."

   Negative Life Pattern: "I must have sex to feel connected."

5. **Care/Nurturing:** This circuit enables us to express empathy, nurturing, and tenderness. Caring is important for affiliating, attaching, and connecting to others. You could call this system your Community Builder.

   Need: To express warmth and empathy toward another, which builds a personal community.

   Positive Life Pattern: "I can care for others and can be cared for."

   Negative Life Pattern: "I can't set boundaries with others" or "I am dependent on others to take care of me as an adult."

6. **Panic:** This emotional circuit activates in response to separation if we have not learned how to be alone. It may be triggered in an emergency situation when a person is in great danger of dying. You could call this system your Lifeguard.

   Need: To maintain affiliation and connectedness.

   Positive Life Pattern: "I can activate in the face of imminent threat."

   Negative Life Pattern: "I will die if the situation becomes slightly threatening."

7. **Play:** This circuit activates the feeling of joy and its expression in laughter. Play eliminates stress and regenerates you with better life balance. A person must feel a sense of safety to activate play. You could call this system your Recreation Director.

   Need: Fun and laughter.

   Positive Life Pattern: "I can see humor in most situations and enjoy playing and having fun."

   Negative Life Pattern: "I can't stop playing computer games" or "I can't be serious."

Take your cue from Gabriella and identify your own life patterns. What do they tell you about your unmet needs? Write down your unmet needs and describe what you think you need to do to meet them.

Because we are not always consciously in charge of our inner states, taking note of what emotional shifts we experience during the day and what circumstances turn on our worry can help us gain more control over our mental states. By learning how to turn on and off emotional circuits, you manage life more easily and diminish your worries. With conditioning, you will be able to activate the right circuits you need to deal with life circumstances.

Apply Neuro-Repatterning

Neuro-repatterning helps you regulate your feelings so they are no longer out of control. Just like learning how to play an instrument or develop an athletic skill, you must practice mentally and physically by building new brain connections. When you have a strong feeling and learn how to reduce its intensity, you loosen the connection of behavior to the feeling. This allows a new positive thought and behavior to connect to the emotional state. Neuro-repatterning can help you change your focus of attention so you shift out of scary and worried thinking, change a dead-end life pattern, and condition your brain to run smoothly.

All seven emotional circuits are important for getting along successfully in the world. Curiosity, Play, Lust, and Nurture, in particular, are antidotes to worry. Fear, Rage, and Panic can be helpful to stimulate you to action when you need to take care of yourself, but they have to be managed so you don't get over-aroused and react inappropriately to situations. Using neuro-repatterning to make even a small adjustment to a negative emotional charge can go a long way toward interrupting a habitual pattern of reactivity.

The Steps

The next time you start to feel worried or upset and find yourself fixated on a mental horror movie about everything that will surely go wrong, start the neuro-repatterning process by asking yourself: What's going on? Why am I so worried about this? Just replacing your worry and fear with curiosity, and taking the time to answer the questions will immediately reduce the intensity of your emotion. It gives you a chance to side-step the negative feeling and shift into one that is easier to manage and more productive.

The next step in neuro-repatterning is to stop moving and take stock of your body. Where do you feel the emotion? Is there pressure anywhere? The answer is likely to be yes, so focus on the pressure and try to remember where or when else you've experienced it. This information can give you clues about why you're reacting the way you are. Remember: As we discussed in Chapter 3, we internalize the moments when our emotions are formed, and so our past informs our current emotional habits and triggers our reactions. Then take a deep breath and exhale several times until you get into a calmer state.

Once you have replaced worry with curiosity, step three is to ask "What do I need?" Let's say you realize that you need to feel nurtured. The appropriate response would be to take steps that could trigger the emotional circuit that will fulfill that need, such as making a pedicure appointment or scheduling a dinner date with your partner, no kids allowed. Once you begin to feel better, you'll be better able to problem-solve.

The fourth step is to mentally call up your Pioneer (Curiosity), Lover (Lust), Community Builder (Care), or your Recreation Director (Play). Ask yourself: What do I want to explore? Who do I want to be sexual with? What group do I want more time with? And what play activities do I want to engage in? Imaging yourself acting on each these desires will help you practice turning on the relevant circuit.

Remember: You cannot hold two emotional states at once. This is a trick you can apply to all kinds of emotions. Humor or play can easily dissipate worry, anger, or fear, which is why one of the best remedies for a bad day is to watch children play and laugh. Just the act of smiling changes your muscles and starts moving your brain circuitry from one state to another. Changing your physiology always changes your mental state, so the idea is to expose yourself to something that won't fuel the circuitry that is causing you pain or trouble. You want to turn on the neurocircuitry that will serve you the best in any situation.

You can also try this exercise when you have a negative thought: Ask: Does this help me? If not, refocus your attention on relaxing your tongue and imagine breathing through your feet. Now ponder your future possibilities without making any negative judgments. Notice the relief you feel. You have just turned down your sympathetic nervous system and turned on a curiosity circuit.

Try It Now

Follow this neuro-repatterning process to recondition your worry to curiosity, self-nurture, or play.

1. Acknowledge your worried state and the issues driving it. Consider times when you feel positive and hopeful. Who are you with and what are you doing?

2. Define your problem in solvable terms. By focusing on shifting a negative reaction rather than running mental serial movies with no ending, you can intervene and manage your emotional states.

3. Identify your target emotional circuit and the mental state you would prefer to act on. This can include accessing your Pioneer (Curiosity), Lover (Lust), Community Builder (Care/Nurturing), or Recreation Director (Play).

4. Move toward the emotional state you want to have. You can use any of the tools we've discussed in this book, such as bilateral stimulation, Mind Wandering, deep state dive, Future Thinking, or neuro-repatterning, to help you. Think about bringing yourself closer to your target state. Just as you might walk on stones across a garden, what do you need to do to move closer to how you want to feel?

5. Condition and reinforce the new emotion by remembering when you last felt it. Discuss how it felt with a friend, and begin to notice when you experience it.
6. Practice this state whenever possible.
7. Notice how, now that you're in a healthier emotional state, your mind is able to develop workable solutions to the problems that used to worry you.
8. Notice when your thinking and perceptions begin to change. How do your interactions with people improve? Do you seem less reactive?
9. Continue to practice the emotional circuit that best interferes with worry.

Plan of Action

Back to Gabriella. After moving through the exercise above, we asked if she was willing to look for the exceptions in her limiting belief that everything was up to her where it might not be true. She was. And that was a coup, because finding her curiosity was the first small step she needed to take to shift out of her frustration and despair. She thought back to when she insisted her siblings help her with their mother, and they finally did.

Second, we asked her to think about what her family truly needed from her, and what she only thought they needed. What could she let go? She thought she could hover over her son less frequently.

Third, she really needed a community centered on something that gave her a sense of pleasure or comfort, such as a cause, a hobby, or a place of worship. Where did Gabriella think she could find a group that would embrace her and make her feel as though she belonged? She loved to paint and joined an artist group that met regularly for social interaction and individual art projects.

Fourth, we suggested she find a mentor. She evaluated her network for someone she could hang out with who was expert at the skills she needed to learn—setting boundaries, asking for help when appropriate, and confronting others when needed. She chose her Sunday School teacher, who frequently presented talks on Eastern psychology and who was both kind and had good personal boundaries.

From the first time Gabriella practiced the neuro-repatterning process she reported feeling comforted and relieved. The curiosity she applied toward figuring out the root of her issues revealed answers she'd never considered, and once she saw them in the light of day, they seemed small and manageable. The future looked brighter to her.

She started dealing with conflict and expressing her needs. Instead of allowing herself to bathe in the Rage circuit when one of her clients had a ridiculous list of demands, she turned on the Play circuit, which helped her keep her good humor. Rather than work harder and keep silent while seething with resentment, she found a gentle way to set a boundary, responding gently, "For the sake of this project, let's figure out what you want and what you need, and go from there. But we have to fit into my time frame. " Her client was taken aback but Gabriella's tone was so warm and confident that he responded, "Sorry, I'm really stressing over this. Let's figure out what is reasonable."

Develop Inner Stability

One thing we really wanted to help Gabriella experience was inner stability. We enter a calmer state when we turn on the emotional circuits appropriate to our environment and circumstances. When your brain is satisfied with this composed state, it begins to stay there longer. The calm mind/body state works well as your default state, the inner place to which you return after an upset or a joyful experience. When you practice switching circuits, you are more in control of yourself, or to use another phrase, you're non-reactive. The resulting inner stability has been described through the centuries as mastery of mind, enlightenment, calm mind, or inner strength.

To get there, much like in martial arts, you begin to find this inner strength physiologically by stabilizing yourself through standing equally on two feet. Then, feel your balanced center 2 inches below the belly button. Imagine you have a powerful energy moving from the universe through the crown of your head, down to the power center located 2 inches below your navel, and then into the earth. When you stand poised in this position, you are stronger. Ask someone to try to push you over. It's impossible. Once you memorize that feeling, you should use it when you feel yourself reacting emotionally: Shift your focus to your power spot 2 inches below your belly button and imagine breathing from there. Your inner power and resolve to stay non-reactive shifts your brain circuits from Fear or Rage to Calm strength. It takes some practice, but once you master this technique it will be hugely effective in helping you stay in control.

Though it is natural to worry at times, and it is great to embrace your feelings, you don't have to stay in the middle of them. Your inner resources construct a personal shield of inner stability. These inner resources might include courage, confidence, clarity, an ability to develop contingencies, or awareness. Carry this shield with you wherever you go. No one will know it's there, but you'll find that negative or problematic situations bounce right off you.

Try It Now

Think of a little worry or something sad (don't go overboard). Now, smile. Hold that smile for one minute. Poof! The worry is gone, right? This is your brain's magic. When you need a quick fix before you go into a meeting or need to have a phone call, smile and notice the giggle that follows. When you change your physiology, your internal state shifts.

If you have trouble shifting circuits, watch an animal video on Facebook. Most of them warm your heart and turn on one of the emotional circuits of Curiosity, Play, or Nurture, which are portals through which empathy and joy occur.

Interpersonal Neuro-Repatterning

Your friends, family, and colleagues respond to your brain's activity. If you function from a closed and inflexible inner state, others will respond in defensiveness and struggle rather than cooperating with you. Conversely, if you are calm and adaptable, others will move toward you in a positive manner.

Healthy relationships help buffer you against bad brain patterns such as meltdowns, or as we like to call them "trips to Freakout Land," and negativity. The more honest your relationships are, the better feedback you receive about how you interact in both positive and negative ways.

As Gabriella reached out to others and set appropriate boundaries with her siblings and clients, her limiting beliefs began to dissolve and her life patterns changed. People invited her to events, her siblings helped with her mother from time to time, and as she took more time for herself, she felt energized and it seemed that she had more time in her day for satisfying work. When her siblings disappointed her by not helping out, Gabriella took it as a minor inconvenience, not a full-blown drama. But she didn't let it slide, either. She let them know that she still expected their participation, and after a while they became much more dependable.

The best measure for intimacy is the frequency of positive interactions you experience with your partner and family, and your mutual willingness to ask for and receive feedback about the quality of your interactions. To measure that quality for yourself, just be aware of which internal states you experience when around others. That is, do you notice more negative reactivity around certain people than others? When you really resonate with someone you feel an easy flow of acceptance and well being; you frequently share laughter. When this happens, it means your brains are in synchrony.

There is evidence of interpersonal neurobiology in all relationships. Everything you say to another person has a neural effect. Emotions tend to be contagious. When we are around negative energy, we start to feel sad or anxious. When we are around upbeat people, our energy rises, our mood is great, and we want to be around that person more frequently. A key to feeling great is to be selective with whom you surround yourself.

Expect the Best

As a person begins to meet needs, change states appropriately, and reprogram life patterns, the world reflects these changes by people reacting differently, and this new response reinforces the new behaviors. Jean Houston, author, scholar, philosopher, and researcher in the human potential movement, reported a conversation she had with Margaret Mead, the famous anthropologist, that sums up what we have discussed in terms of needs, beliefs, and life patterns. Jean told Margaret that she seemed incredibly lucky; really wonderful things always seemed to happen to her. What was her secret? Margaret replied matter-of-factly, "I expect them to."

In a nutshell:

1. Curiosity calms Fear, so ask yourself what you are really afraid of when you're fearful.
2. Play, which includes humor, changes anger. When it is appropriate, try to see the humor in a situation that may be making you angry.
3. Empathy shifts Anger and Fear. Practice nurturing yourself or another person before if you begin to react negatively to your thoughts or their words or behavior.
4. Deep breathing calms Anxiety and a worried mind unless you allow yourself to get to an emotional state where you can't calm yourself down, so practice breathing early and often when you feel the slightest hint of the worry movie starting up in your mind.
5. The key to a successful life is learning to modulate your emotions by knowing how to trigger your emotional circuits at will.

Power Thought: *When you learn to replace one emotion with another, you can get your needs met and gain a sense of control over your life, so there's no need to worry. Ever.*

———————

Profound change is possible when we learn to shift our brain circuitry from ones that hold us back to those that serve us well, practicing the states associated with those circuits, fulfilling our needs, and creating an environment that reinforces our optimal states of being. In addition, these processes help balance life by clearing frantic activity and making time for self-care activities such as the ones we will discuss in Chapter 7.

CHAPTER 7

Neuro-Wellness Rituals to Break Through Crises

Worry often gives a small thing a big shadow.
—Swedish Proverb

After two years of nursing his wife through her cancer treatments and checking in on his elderly parents, Jack feels like he's about to break. So much about his life is good, and Jack is grateful—especially now that his wife is in remission—but he's worried that life is slipping by and he's not making the most out of it. He's afraid that he's missing out on some essential element of happiness. There's an inexplicable echo in the back of his mind, an ache for..something. Well aware of how quickly one's health can turn for the worse, he's worried that he may not have time to discover what that something is, and he's feeling every tick of the clock.

Is your worry about what might have been standing in the way of having a deeper connection to what is? To the people you love? To a deeper meaning to life? This chapter will help you relieve your worry by helping you use a neuro-wellness process that allows you to listen deeply to your yearnings and desires, appreciate what you have, and clear a path toward a no-regrets life.

Neuro-Wellness Allows Us to Enjoy Life

You don't have to be dealing with a crisis like Jack's to forget to take care of yourself. Our culture almost demands it. Many people are so busy achieving their goals and taking care of others that they neglect themselves, forgoing exercise, vacations, hobbies, and even family time so they can squeeze every last minute of productivity out of their day. But as we get older and face empty nests or retirement, many of us worry about our mortality, about whether we've made the right choices, about whether "this" is all there is, and about whether we'll have time to recapture all the dreams we put aside. Worries like these have caused many a mid-life crisis. Head them off at the pass with self-care rituals of neuro-wellness, a tool that helps you create a sense of connection to yourself and takes your brain out of its busy Beta state into the placid, contented Alpha comfort. Self-care can be as simple as sitting alone in your favorite chair with a book or walking the dog. It's any activity whose only purpose is to make you relaxed, calm, and more connected to life. Worry naturally subsides during these exercises. The more you incorporate these rituals into daily life, the more you condition your mind to stay in calmer states even under stress.

How Neuro-Wellness Yields Insight

Jack's demanding and stressful situation had led him into the kind of existential crisis that most of us eventually experience in some form. Illness, the demands of providing food and shelter, and tragedy are a part of even the happiest life, and they can often make us question our choices and reevaluate our assumptions about and plans for the future. When Jack came to us, he had many conflicting feelings. On one hand he wanted to take care of his wife, but on the other hand he resented that some of his needs weren't being met, and he was worried that his existence would be defined in unending caregiving. At this time in his life he had thought he'd be furthering his education and starting his own business, but those plans were now on hold. He didn't have the energy to take on coursework, nor could he take the risk of not having a salary. He was also disappointed that he and his wife couldn't take any of the trips they'd once planned.

We encouraged Jack to talk about his frustration and reassured him that his uncomfortable feelings were normal. As he spoke, tears welled up in his eyes while he released the pent-up tension he could not share with his wife because of her weakened condition. We asked Jack to talk about the trips he'd wanted to take with his wife and what those adventures might have done for his relationship. He said it would have been romantic and would have brought them closer. We asked him to think about how he felt as he was taking care of his wife during the worst of her illness. He paused and said, "I felt very close to her and didn't want to lose her." The worry over losing her had heightened his awareness of how important she was to him. Jack realized that while no one would wish his wife's illness on anyone, in the midst of a scary and demanding situation, he had experienced the very core of what he wanted to feel with his wife: intimacy. Jack fondly remembered how the two of them gazed at each other when he would tend to her, deepening a sense of their love. Finding a safe place with us to vent his frustrations had also allowed him to recognize that some good might have come from the whole ordeal, but he was worried that life would pass him by. His personal needs were not being met.

Jack felt exhausted. Worse yet, he felt under threat from potentially being alone and worried about not getting to live his life. We asked him to consider what he'd need to regain his energy and to feel fulfilled. Some time alone, he replied emphatically. He had not taken any time for himself since his wife had gotten sick. We weren't surprised. People often become hyper-focused when they find themselves in the midst of a crisis that demands their intense attention. Jack worried that he had lost himself in the process of trying hard to be loving and supportive. The fear and sense of personal responsibility can become so great that we may not ask for assistance from friends, family, or neighbors. And we can become so used to living this way that even when circumstances improve, we may still have a difficult time recalibrating and broadening our focus of attention. Jack wondered if now might be a good time to try.

We suggested he take a week off and sign up for a meditation retreat where he could focus on himself, catch up on sleep, and come to terms with his worry thoughts and feelings that time might be running out for him. But he had used up too much of his employer's good will; he wasn't comfortable asking for yet more time off. That was fine, we assured him. Even taking a single weekend morning off by himself would be a step in the right direction of neuro-wellness.

To achieve neuro-wellness, we have to allow ourselves to engage in the kind of self-care exercises that reduce stress, change unhealthy patterns, and create synergy among the mind, body, and brain. Jack could do whatever he liked—take a walk, see a movie, head to the gym, have breakfast with friends—so long as it was entirely pleasant and stress-free. In addition, it was imperative that Jack slow down, even just for a few minutes per day, and meditate. A few minutes of daily meditation promotes the healthiest states of mind. When you can be fully in the present without judgment or expectation—which is the goal of most meditation practice—you minimize suffering and stress and become more aware of what makes you feel alive.

We offered Jack two meditation strategies. The first is called "coherent breathing" a tool to bring both the sympathetic system and parasympathetic system into balance and that results in a synchrony of Alpha frequency throughout the brain. It takes very little time to make you feel great. It's not very hard: Sit straight with good posture, relax the face, jaw, chin, and tongue, and slow your breathing to six seconds of inhalation, belly out, followed by six seconds of exhalation, belly in. Immediately you will begin to create profound relaxation. Within one cycle of coherent breathing (six seconds inhalation, six seconds, exhalation) the amplitudes of Alpha immediately rise.[1] Once you feel calm, imagine breathing through your heart while remembering someone or something you care about deeply. The research clearly shows this approach quickly leads to inner balance.[2]

The second meditation breathing exercise Jack could have tried was called the "relaxation response," devised by Herbert Benson of the Harvard Medical School. It is useful in longer meditations. This one is not hard, either: Sit in a relaxed position, and with your eyes closed visualize the number 1 on your mental screen. As you exhale slowly, imagine the 1 moving farther out into the distance. As you breathe in, bring the 1 back to the forefront. Your mind will chatter, so let your thoughts come and go, but keep gently bringing your mind back to the number 1. Start practicing this exercise for five minutes a day and work up to 20 minutes.[3] Your mind's chatter will eventually slow down.

Meditation naturally moves the mind to a place of greater joy and connection, and decreases the frequency of worry—because our emotions develop according to what we pay attention to. Paying attention to negative experiences makes them bigger; paying attention to positive experiences expands their intensity and frequency (or rather, our ability to notice them). Taking the time to notice small things like the feel of the breeze on our skin or noticing our breath as it gently comes in and goes out places our attention in the present moment and displaces worry thoughts.

With his wife's blessing, Jack slept late the following weekend and spent most of rest of his time reading inspirational literature. He also began a daily meditation practice. The next time we saw him, he had found new perspective. He realized how precious his time with his wife had become. Though it was painful to deal with her treatment and worry around losing her, for him the real meaning in life was to relate, connect, and share intimate experiences with family, even if the time he had might be shorter than he hoped. This was his purpose beyond what money he could make, or things he could acquire, or accolades he might win. But he had also become aware that his needs for creative self-expression weren't getting met. He had always wanted to be a sculptor. As a young man he had focused on his artistry and won many awards, but the demands of life had made him put his pursuit on the back burner. He didn't realize how not expressing himself had creatively dulled his spirit and increased his worry. Without a personal creative pursuit, his tendency was to hover over his wife. She was doing much better, though, and with his new perspective, Jack began to think about how he could make some adjustments and incorporate his passion back into his own life.

Focus on You to Change Your Future

Like Jack, having too many responsibilities can numb you to daily life and cause you to dissociate in order to function in the world. You might not realize it, but when you're overwhelmed your feelings and body sensations dampen, and your joyful moments disappear, giving more room for worry to set in and giving negative events greater meaning. Engaging in self-care rituals of neuro-wellness helps us create deep connections and lessens our need to worry, generating subtle changes that transform and shift us into the best version of ourselves. It allows you to begin to recognize small opportunities that show up and signal the opening of a new future. You start to act from your best future self, and your present becomes the future you imagined with less worry about how to create it. That's what happened to Jack. He set up his own sculpting studio, and with new excitement, he began a new project. Three months later, he began to seriously think about developing his own business.

Try It Now

The following self-care activities condition and rewire the brain through a repatterning process to turn off worry, recapture a life's passion, experience an anti-stress health boost, get in touch with unmet needs, and turn off the mental horror movies. The more positive you are, the more you activate neural pathways that lead you to think and take action toward the positive futures you imagine.

1. Drink a cup of tea. Both black and green teas con-
    tain the amino acid L-theanine, which stimulates
    the Alpha frequency in the brain and leads to a
    calm but mentally alert state. Sit back and enjoy
    the warmth and quiet feeling that comes over you
    and ask the question, "What is my passion?"
2. Sit in front of running water. Ideally, of course,
    your source of running water would be something
    beautiful like a lake, river, or ocean, but a small
    indoor fountain will work, too. Even merely look-
    ing at a picture of water can soothe your body and
    mind and turn on your Alpha frequency, which
    takes your mind away from worry and puts it into
    a state of ease. Ask the question "How can I free
    up time for myself?"
3. Shake a snowglobe. You can make your own by
    filling a Mason jar with water and sprinkling glit-
    ter into it. Stress always narrows our ideas of
    what is possible; this exercise helps you relax and
    recognize that you're never as stuck as you think
    you are. As you watch the snowflakes gently fall
    to the bottom, imagine the snow is your worry
    thoughts settling down. The mind tends to notice
    negative thoughts before positive ones, so by mov-
    ing your negative thoughts out of the way to the
    bottom of the snowglobe, you can make room for
    more positive thoughts and change the content of
    your mind. As your breathing slows, your relax-
    ation-Alpha state switch will turn on. Each time
    you use your "mind globe," you gracefully rein-
    vent what's possible by resetting access to your
    internal resources. While you are playing with the
    snowglobe, ask the question "What are the possi-
    bilities for my life that I have not yet considered?"

    Remember: You must have relaxation expe-
    riences each day to deactivate the 1,200 stress

genes that can turn on chronic illness. These calm positive moments also strengthen the neural pathways that lead to better health and peak performance, which we discuss in Chapter 9.

4. Watch a flock of birds flying in formation. As they soar over your head, marvel at how they know to fly perfectly equidistant from each other. Watching the synchronized pattern of a flock of flying birds is mesmerizing, causing us to focus our attention and relax. Birds as well as other mammals produce and sense magnetic fields that guide their flight. It's not magnetic, but the inner compass you carry within you can also help you know what path to take; achieving stillness will allow you to access it. Ask the question "What path is right for me now?"

5. Make it a point to be around happy people on a regular basis. Our bodies release oxytocin, the bonding chemical, when we're having fun. Laughter releases tension, creates connections with others, and turns on our Play circuit and increases Alpha. Your brain models or entrains to the emotional states in others. Ask the question "What makes me laugh?"

6. Eating your meals more slowly will increase your ability to taste the subtle flavors of food. Use whole foods and good nutrition to feed your cells the electricity and nutrients they need. The most recent research demonstrates that the content of your mind moves more toward happiness as the quality of the food you eat improves.[4] Ask the question "How do I feel after I eat something?"

7. Exercise regularly. Physical activity stabilizes your mood, tones your muscles, and makes you feel good physically and mentally. It calms the mind and lifts worry better than placebos or antidepressants. When performed three times per week, aerobic and weightlifting exercise can inoculate you from worry and stress. Ask the question

"How great is the mellow feeling I get after exercising and how long does it last?"

8. Expose yourself to sunlight. New research suggests that our bodies give off photons of light that reflect its level of health.[5] The body needs to be nourished with sunlight to increase its own production of light and vitamin D. Because we tend to work and live in cave-like dwellings away from natural light, take daytime walks outdoors several times a week. People who don't exercise tend to have more worry, anxiety, and low vitamin D; taking a walk in sunlight makes you feel happier and nourishes your body. Ask the question "How do I feel after taking a walk in the sunshine?"

9. Begin your day with inspiring thoughts and gratitude. This practice can set your internal state in a positive direction for an entire day. By intentionally listing the many life-gifts available rather than reviewing the dark forces demonstrated through violence in the world, you shift your awareness to what is wonderful. Inspiration puts you into the zone, develops fascination, and helps you transcend worry when possibilities suddenly become illuminated. J.K. Rowling once said in an interview that the image of Harry Potter with the lightning scar on his forehead zapped her out of the blue, and provided the inspiration to work out the story.[6] Your fascination with an idea can become your crystal ball for an invention.

10. Meditate daily. Any kind of meditation is helpful for teaching yourself to stay calm and chase away unwanted worry thoughts when they try to take root. In his research exploring how meditation affects self-care, neuroscientist Richard Davidson at the University of Wisconsin found that it spurs many physical responses: The sympathetic nervous system quiets, blood pressure

decreases, and the immune response increases. People who meditate can experience many psychological changes as well. They might feel less angry, have more empathy, take less interest in drinking alcohol, find themselves less emotionally reactive and describe themselves as happier. Above all, his subjects reported that the distressing thoughts that would loop around and around in their minds disappeared.[7]

One of the most exciting studies at the University of Virginia's School of Medicine found that stressful thoughts and feelings affect our immune systems by increasing inflammation that leads to chronic disease. In a 2012 paper, Jonathan Kipnis and his team outlined their findings that there is a unique interplay between the central nervous system and the immune system. Specifically, fearful emotional states that you keep reliving from the past can inflame the body and set up potential chronic illness.[8] According to a five-year Harvard study on meditation, you can also simply meditate on a word that captures one of your deepest personal values. Repeating the word will turn off genes that stimulate the inflammatory response. The word might be *calm*, *peace*, or *confident*.[9] Ask the question, "Which meditation word works best for me?"

11. Turn your body into a personal biofeedback system. By checking in regularly with yourself several times per day, for example at 10 a.m., 2 p.m., and 4 p.m., you'll notice stressful thoughts or body tension before they get out of control, and can then remind yourself to stay calm and engage in any of the previous exercises to maintain your sense of stability and stay in the best physical and mental states possible. Ask the question "What are the worry thoughts that disappear when I allow them to leave at these particular times?"

Find Your Pause Button

Sometimes we forgo self-care because we feel like we're just too busy, but often we actively damage our bodies by leaning on addictive behaviors or substances to help us cope with a life shock. And sometimes our addictions can actually cause the life shock. Whether it's to food, drink, sex, or anything else, addiction will clobber you with its consequences. The only upside is that once you hit rock bottom, and you will, it, like all other life shocks, it will give you the opportunity for deep self-examination. But if you don't have a full-blown addiction yet, you can choose to make a change before you're hit with devastating results, like starting to drink alcohol before late afternoon. It's about developing what Pamela Peeke, assistant professor of medicine at the University of Maryland, author, food addiction expert, and long-time meditator, calls an internal pause button. If you can use one to delay an impulse, such as overeating or drinking, you are less likely to follow through on the thought.[10]

Good habit-forming self-care like exercise and meditation can help develop your internal pause button. Exercise teaches you to put mind over matter when you feel discomfort, or distracts you from it altogether. It feels great (when you're done) in the short term, and it gives you confidence as you look and feel better over time. Meditation teaches you to notice how your sensations arise and fade without judgment, or telling yourself a story, which fades worry and changes your thinking over time. Exercise and meditation teach you to notice your thoughts without acting on them, which gives you a greater ability to hit the pause button. For example, let's say you have a thought that something is wrong with you physically. You can begin to worry and ruminate about this potential problem but choose not to visit your physician. Meditation reduces stress and keeps reactivity at bay. You will be more likely to follow through with checking out a worrisome symptom without ruminating on it. Then, you acknowledge the thoughts, make a plan of action, and let the worry thoughts pass. When a worry thought rises, because you enjoy a calmer mind you learned from training the mind, you let it go.

In addition, exercise and meditation can enhance your energy, drive, creativity, and introspection, which increases your happiness. This decreases your worries, which increases your ability to stay in control of your life. By doing any of the neuro-wellness activities of self-care, you repattern your brain to turn on different neural circuits. As these neural pathways activate, they help you regain the internal resources that allow you to believe Winnie-the-Pooh's wise words: You're braver than you believe, and stronger than you seem, and smarter than you think.

A lot of worry stems from fear of the unknown. But as Joseph Campbell said, "We must be willing to get rid of the life we've planned, so as to have the life that is waiting for us."[11] Here again, self-care can help. It doesn't have to be physical activity. It could involve changing your diet, leaving a dysfunctional relationship, changing a dead-end job, or giving up knocking on a closed door to get into the "in" crowd. If you can face your worry that things might be worse than the way things are, and jump into the risky abyss of change, doors can open that you would never have anticipated. By leaving something familiar, there is always regret. Moving into something new always provides both anticipation and awkwardness until the new becomes familiar. At their most effective, meditation and exercise can give us access to the deeper aspects of the self.

Deep Self

The deep self is that psychological, philosophical, and spiritual dimension innate in all humans that expresses itself in wisdom and understanding. As Jack became calm, the nature of his worry dissolved because he no longer saw the world in dualities. His choice was no longer to either take care of his wife and sacrifice everything he wanted to do, or live out his dream. By being willing to accept his own struggle and frustration, Jack realized a number of things. One was that there is great meaning in mundane and demanding caretaking chores. Two, taking care of his wife didn't mean he needed to exhaust himself beyond reason. Three, he could find help from others and free up his time to focus on his own creative and spiritual needs. The growth that he could find in self-care activities energized him and allowed more intimacy between Jack and his wife. He discovered an inner compass that was freed from either-or thinking and his worry began to melt away.

Lack of worry didn't mean he no longer had any concerns, of course. But he felt more confident in his ability to cope with them. His new mindset—feeling connected to his deeper self and to others, recapturing his creative spark, and integrating a sense of internal purpose—allowed him to move toward creative actions and out of a compulsive worry loop. He was finally functioning as the person he had always wanted to be.

Deep Listening

As Jack began to slow himself down, he listened to his inner desires and noticed the signals his body was giving when he was tired. Before the meditation, he could not honor his own physical signals and respond appropriately. We call this process "deep listening," and it helps you connect with the deeper aspects of your self. Deep listening is being curious about your thoughts and feelings without judgment or trying to control or change them. By using a respectful inner ear, you witness your thoughts and feelings. If you have never given yourself this kind of attention, it may be difficult at first to be gracious with yourself and just listen. If you're reading this book, your usual habit is probably to debate, argue, and struggle with your thoughts and feelings, and then worry about them. But if you can move into a deeper place inside yourself and really listen in a contemplative frame of mind, you will begin to respect yourself more. You can even respect your worry thoughts more without self-criticism. When you engage in deep listening through meditation, you often become conscious that you've been holding on to old limiting ideas. That awareness allows you to release the worry and stop struggling. As a result, you can be more relaxed and caring toward yourself.

Bill was once asked to lead a meditation at a Buddhist temple. He started the group out with a simple exercise of focusing on their breath. There was no air circulating in the room, and he became quite warm and began to perspire. As he started to sweat more profusely, he had a difficult time keeping his attention focused on his breathing. Bill became anxious and worried that he wasn't modeling the meditation correctly. The more he worried that he wasn't doing the exercise right, the more he perspired, and the more he struggled to focus. He began to fight internally with his own body signals.

Finally, Bill realized that he could change his mental state by changing his focus and thus his emotional circuit. He mentally followed the beads of sweat pouring down his face and thought the word *sweating*. This focus enabled him to relax and not fight the perspiration. In his mind's eye, he observed the sweat as it rolled down his head, eventually falling on the nape of his neck. As it did this, he felt a slight chill. Had he been in a struggle with his thoughts, he wouldn't have noticed the more pleasant feeling of coolness. He observed his body temperature alternating between very warm and cool. By shifting his focus, he no longer identified with someone who was uncomfortable and unable to follow his breath, so there was no struggle. Letting go of worry and the internal fight led to an insight. By turning on the emotional circuit of Curiosity (see Chapter 6), Bill dissolved his worry about not doing things correctly and his sweating, and his physiology, changed dramatically. By listening deeply to his sensations and thoughts without reacting to them, he completely changed the experience.

There is a fine line between dissociating from a sensation or blocking it out, and just observing what is happening. When we dissociate from something like pain, it may be more difficult to pay close enough attention and take appropriate action to care for ourselves physically. For example, prior to developing a meditation practice, Bill had begun to experience shoulder pain. His athletic background was permeated by the philosophy of "no pain, no gain," with coaching instructions to worry if he wasn't pushing himself beyond his limits. Hearing his former coaches' voices in his head about it being important to drive yourself, Bill chose to ignore the discomfort he felt in his shoulder. He would dissociate from it and continue to go to the gym to lift weights. For a long time it was easy to dissociate from the pain, especially when he warmed up and the adrenaline began flowing. Eventually, however, he exercised in a way that turned an inflammation into a tear. Bill's personal story that he should exercise through the pain enabled the dissociation and made the situation worse until he had no choice but to have surgery. When you don't use deep listening with regard to your body, worry sometimes leads to poor decisions.

When you listen deeply to your desires and settle your worried mind, you can more easily see the future you want to live. And when you imagine a specific future, you are more likely to have creative ideas about how to embrace that future. Artists, musicians, businesspeople, inventors, and entrepreneurs do it all the time, guided by an inner knowledge that brings creativity into actuality. When this happens, it's as if the music writes itself; the painting paints itself, and creative ideas pop into the mind like someone else whispered the thought. From his research with advanced fakirs in India, Dale Walters, a psychologist who worked with Elmer Green, father of biofeedback at Menninger's in the 1970s, believes it is possible that this information comes from our connection to a universal "field of information" that is shared between and a part of every human being alive. He posited that intuition is actually our brains recalling information it has gleaned across time and space from the collective unconscious.[12] Listening deeply to your intuition connects you to all that is, thus providing a strong sense of security. It's why people with strong intuitions don't worry about the things they intuit as much as those who don't trust or pay much attention to theirs.

One of our clients struggled with her heightened intuition. She was able to feel people's pain when she shared the same space with them, such as at church or the office. This experience was so uncomfortable for her that she actually felt physical pain. She worried that picking up on others' feelings would become unbearable. Knowing that empaths (people with high intuitive ability) have dominant Theta waves, we suggested she let us hook her up to our EEG system to check her brain out. Sure enough, with her eyes open she produced more Theta than any other brain frequency. We knew the key to her feeling more comfortable was to learn how to regulate this slow brain frequency. She learned to use deep listening, which would give her the ability to allow information in when she wanted it, and an ability to leave it out when she didn't.

The only problem with teaching her how to manage her dominant brain waves better was the risk of losing her intuitive ability if she didn't stay with the mental training she did at home. Her positive premonitions had led her to make good decisions in many areas of life, and she wanted to keep her internal guide.

To start, we suggested that she notice what happened to her mind when she focused on mundane activities like reconciling her bank account or grocery shopping with a list, which should lower the slow frequency amplitudes and raise her Beta brain waves. In fact, this activity lessened her intuitive ability. She practiced switching her focus of attention back and forth to a cognitive activity and then to a state of intuitive receptiveness until she felt more in control of her attention. She practiced making a mental grocery list and then shifting into a deeply relaxed state to tune into another person in the same room with her. If she noticed feeling discomfort from feeling another person's pain, she moved her attention away. Her own deep listening to her levels of comfort became a signal for shifting attention. She learned how to control her focus of attention just like changing radio stations. As she learned how to be in control of tuning in to others, the discomfort disappeared, and she developed more flexibility in shifting states through the act of deep listening.

Design New Adventures

Joseph Campbell said, "I don't believe people are looking for the meaning of life as much as they are looking for the experience of being alive."[13] Besides taking important self-care breaks, you can keep worries and insecurities at bay by giving yourself interesting and novel experiences. Exploring new places, different cultures, philosophies, or subjects of interests can enliven your life and expand your mind. What have you done in the past to feel alive, and what new adventures would you would like to have? If you have no clue, try a new adventure for a start, maybe something you always wanted to do but never dared. It will raise your level of excitement and give you newfound energy.

Self-Connection and Shared Connection

Self-connection gives you more choice over your internal states, perspectives, and personal decisions, shutting down worry. It also allows you to become hyper-aware of your sensations and surroundings, expanding your feeling of being fully alive.

If you have ever had the experience of communicating with a pet, you can feel touched with affection and appreciation. When our cat wants us to wake up in the morning, she gently jumps on the bed, comes over to one of us, and carefully puts her paw lightly on one closed eye. This is shared connection. When you have intimate moments of connection, you develop a deep sense of being connected to all that is. When you worry, you separate yourself from connection.

One of our self-care practices is to gaze at a picture of the ocean at Esalen in Big Sur, California, on our computer. We can feel the shift to a calm mind whenever we look at it.

The scene reminds us of meeting a photographer, Andy, at Esalen when we were teaching there. Andy had an amazing experience sailing in his boat one day. It was something he did whenever he was was worried about anything. One day when he was struggling with a financial concern, he took his boat out in the ocean to take some photographs. A beautiful white whale surfaced ever so quietly next to him. It was stunning to see this huge creature. Then the whale moved around to see Andy clearly and looked deep into his eyes. It was one of those astounding moments of intimate connection that could never have been anticipated. Then the whale submerged. Andy noticed that his worry thoughts disappeared in the moment. The experience caused him to suspend his habitual pattern of worrying about money, redirect attention to this amazing encounter and later to the inner source of his upset, and let go of a habitual worry thought. It occurred to him to begin looking for these moments of connection in nature. As he took a number of photographs of these encounters, his photography business bloomed, and his financial concerns subsided. The most popular photos he sold were the whale looking at him and a variety of other intimate nature moments of animals connecting, and birds communicating with humans.

He kept going out in the ocean for months in hopes of seeing his new friend again. One day, when Andy was busy photographing the surrounding cliffs from his boat, a whale surfaced next to his vessel. He had the familiar coloring around his eyes that made Andy immediately recognize him. Andy smiled and said, "Hello, old friend. Nice to see you again." Again he had that moment of connection, and eye-to-eye meeting that now communicated a sense of safe familiarity. This was an intimate moment. The awareness that ultimately you are connected with all things inoculates you against intense concerns, particularly when you feel all alone in a sea of worry. But the process of suspending an old way of thinking and redirecting attention to your inner stillness allows you to let go into a new way of paying attention without the worry.

Follow Your Heart

One day we were strolling along the River Walk in downtown San Antonio, a favorite place of ours, and by chance we stopped by an interesting shop that sold paintings, sculptures, and carvings. A carved wooden green dragon with scales and very long legs caught our attention. In Asian culture, the dragon is a symbol for the unconscious mind and protector of the individual. On the bottom of one foot was stamped a black sheep. We asked the storekeeper about the sculptor. He told us the artist was a young woman who grew up quite poor. Her family struggled with making ends meet, and they couldn't support her heart's calling to create beautiful art objects. The artist worried about disappointing her family, but worse, she really worried about disappointing herself. Her family wanted more security in her life than they had, and art wasn't dependable. The artist yearned to support herself through her art, but she worried that her family was right; she would never make it. She went back and forth mentally over whether she should even try. But her desire to create was incredibly strong. So she snuck out of the house to create her designs. All the animals she carved had extremely long legs stamped with a black sheep. The long legs symbolized that you can rise above your troubles, and the black sheep was a reminder that even if you don't fit in with your "tribe" you can always find a way to follow your heart and be successful. In following your heart, you move into deeper aspects of yourself. This artist set her worry aside, followed her heart's desire, and became a popular sculptor.

Through the neuro-wellness exercises of self-care, mental training, and realizing your mind is really unlimited, you can become aware when worry holds you back from where you want to be in life. After you engage in some of these self-care rituals, don't be disappointed if your mind goes back to your old worries. If that happens, repeat the rituals.

If you notice your thinking is out of whack again, try to name it. You can call it your "worry brain" or "funky thoughts," or whatever you like. If you name your internal chatter before you get to the "uh-oh-here-comes-something-really-bad" response that sends your worry brain into the stratosphere, you'll be able to better control your reaction. If you name the worry brain something funny, like "We're off to see the Wizard," you will immediately change your state, which will make your worry disappear, because you've put a space between your worry thought and your emotional reaction to it, giving you time to find a new response.

Generative Conversation

Taking time to rest and regenerate with individual self-care rituals is crucial to feeling alive, aware, and more present in your life. But these rituals work even better when you also collaborate with others. Connecting with others through conversation activates energy between people that stimulates ideas, feelings, awareness, and a sense of comfort. The conversation becomes generative; that is, it is a shared dialogue leading to the stimulation of more creative possibilities and sources of value. Our friends often give us new ideas and are always important to well-being.

Talking with others is another form of self-care because it promotes deeper understandings, connections, and perspectives that lead to acceptance (including of oneself), reflection, and being open to possibility. The focus is to listen with curiosity and examine suggestions to see what might fit your positive movement toward the future. When you have conversations that generate possibilities, you feel supported.

Power Thought: *Calming your worries through neuro-wellness exercises of self-care allow you to become more present to yourself.*

You have moved into deeper self-inquiry and focused on developing a deeper awareness of yourself, and what makes you feel alive. By taking the time for self-care, you enable profound experiences and self-acceptance that will sustain you in difficult times.

In the next chapter, we will look at how you keep your best internal states going and how to use an amazing key to align your mind, body, and heart.

PART IV

Ignite Your Life

CHAPTER 8

Banish Worry for Good With the Whole Brain State

People become attached to their burdens sometimes
more than the burdens are attached to them.
—George Bernard Shaw

In chapters 1 to 3 you learned how to rewire your brain in a fairly short period of time and interrupt your habitual negative worry patterns. In chapters 4 and 5 you used neuro-association to link certain mental states to behavior patterns, and chapters 6 and 7 introduced you to neuro-repatterning, which helps you practice turning on and off your emotional circuits for mental flexibility. Now, how do you sustain your progress and inoculate against future worry episodes? How can you develop what we call a mastery mind, meaning that rather than merely relieve symptoms of worry, you literally worry very little and instead live more often in the optimal mental states that promote daily performance, creativity, presence, and happiness? Through brain synchrony. What is that? Let's explore it in the natural world.

Synchrony in the Natural World

Anything that moves has a rhythm, and when two or more rhythmic objects or entities come together, their rhythms will eventually match. Sooner or later, the pendulums on two grandfather clocks in the same room will start to swing in the same direction at the same time. Ticking metronomes sitting on a table together will begin to move at the same time. Crickets chirp together as if singing in a choir. Schools of fish swim in coordination, swarms of bacteria move as a single organism, and birds fly in formation. When two pacemaker heart cells are placed in close proximity, they begin beating together. Soldiers marching together over a bridge may cause such coordinated vibration that the bridge collapses. Couples unconsciously mirror each other as they respond to each other. Mothers and children coordinate their gestures and sounds.

History of the Whole Brain State

In the 1960s Joe Kamiya, researcher for the University of California at San Francisco in the Langley-Porter Psychiatric Institute, discovered that Alpha brain waves not only create wonderful feelings of well-being but even transcendent experiences. Kamiya used biofeedback systems to train students how to produce more Alpha frequency. Richard Bach, author of *Jonathan Livingston Seagull*, was an early student; his training culminated in the popular hero's journey story about a seagull whose driving desire was to become all that he could be. Later, Les Fehmi, researcher and director of the Princeton Biofeedback Centre, found that when the brain's activity is synchronized in one or more areas it allows for a broad exchange of information, enabling it to achieve better perception and greater clarity of mind, with less anxiety and effort. Even minor physical pain tends to diminish in intensity and frequency.[1]

Fehmi found that as we grow up, we are conditioned to over-rely on the Beta state. Beta runs 12 to 35 Hertz, and is used to accomplish cognitive tasks. It also frequently reflects tension. The American cultural belief is that the more effort you put out to force something to happen, the more likely you will succeed. But if we can learn to rely on the Alpha frequency instead, success comes more easily.

Because Kamiya's biofeedback approach took at least 20 minutes or more, Fehmi set out to find a quicker way to train students in Alpha, a challenge because it is not a frequency that responds to our command. He discovered that the answer is this: To increase Alpha, don't try; instead, let go. We in the West are not accustomed to letting go, to empty space, or to silence. We talk a lot, we acquire too much, and we often live in clutter. This environment partly helps keep us in a state of Beta because it creates worry and strain. Eastern traditions, however, are constructed to promote Alpha. The Japanese concept of *ma*, which means emptiness or blankness, is reflected in simple spaces and lines in houses and gardens. Clutter in a space leads to higher Beta and tension; simple lines and spaces promote a calmer mind. Buddhist traditions direct meditators to focus on the space in a mandala, and the result of this focus on "nothing" calms the central nervous system. Paying attention to the space between things resets the neural networks by flooding the whole brain with synchronous Alpha, which calms the brain and shuts out worry. The result is more flexible processing and feelings of lightness, well-being, and creativity. Anna Wise, co-director of the Evolving Institute, studied with C. Maxwell Cade, a biofeedback researcher in Britain who observed advanced meditators, and found they produced a unique brain-wave pattern he termed the "awakened mind," another term for the whole brain state. Not only were these meditators completely free of worry during their practice, their calm generalized to their actions, behaviors, and reactions in their everyday lives. Wise defined the awakened mind state as "being in the state you want to be in, when you want to be there, knowing what to do with that state, and being able to accomplish it.[2]

Wise decided to teach students how to replicate the mind of a monk with Cade's biofeedback device, the mind mirror. She and Cade concentrated on increasing the students' Alpha frequency and then balancing the other brain waves. They discovered that almost anyone could develop an awakened mind, or whole brain state, free of worry.

During Cade's era, the technology was only capable of measuring brain waves up to about 30 Hertz, which mapped the awakened mind state. Later the EEG measuring equipment became so sophisticated that a higher Beta frequency was discovered called Gamma, and researchers found that it, too, was produced in bursts by the whole brain state. Recently, studies done on Tibetan Buddhist monks and Celestine nuns demonstrated their ability to produce a whole functioning brain state—synchronous Alpha with bursts of Gamma—during meditation on compassion. The advanced meditators showed a significant increase in brain activity in the left prefrontal cortex, with much less activity in the amygdala, the brain's radar for potential threat. This pattern is associated with self-regulation, happiness, and compassion. The results suggest that when practiced regularly, meditation, especially what we call compassion meditation, or meditating on empty space, promotes Alpha synchrony and can speed the brain toward developing the whole brain state.

Try It Now

Sit in a relaxed position and close your eyes. Focus on feeling love and compassion toward yourself. Experience how space gently permeates everything comfortably. The space in the room, the space in your house, and the space around your house is always present, and by focusing on it you begin to shift into the whole brain state.

Each atom in the body is mostly space. Every area in the body contains space. Focus on the space between your fingers and then your toes. Go inside and focus on the imaginary space in your stomach, chest, arms, legs, and back. Shift your attention to the imaginary space in the body around your heart. When your internal chatter slows down, you'll know that you shifted brain frequencies and created a calmer state. You may notice that in this exercise there is absolutely no worry thought.

Achieving the whole brain state leads to a deeper understanding and mastery of your self. It builds your ability to recover from and inoculates you against life stressors. It's a state where you can easily access information and achieve great insight. You understand your needs, vulnerabilities, yearning, and desires, but they do not control you. In the whole brain state there is no room for worry or rumination or any other negative emotion. It is a state of mind that is more flexible in thinking and clearer than other ordinary states. In fact, the secret to living a worry-free life is practicing the whole brain state.

But to get to that whole brain state, you need to achieve Alpha synchrony.[3]

Alpha Synchrony in the Whole Brain State

When there is synchrony, blood flow equalizes in both hemispheres. The result is emotional balance, which improves our ability to solve complex problems, achieve better understanding and clearer perceptions, and take appropriate actions.[4] Worry, however, tends to block the synchronization of the brain's hemispheres. Worry drags the brain through mental sludge so that the "gears" don't allow the normal hemispheric shift from left to right and back again to occur with ease. This can impede your brain's ability to process information, which stalls your problem-solving capabilities. As your brain tries to come up with solutions by worrying, it's actually stuck in place, like a truck spinning its wheels fruitlessly in the mud. In addition, an imbalanced brain that doesn't communicate well can be dangerous to your health. One of the newer ideas in neuroscience being explored in the United Kingdom and Russia is that the body's physiological systems are synchronized by brain-wave frequency.[5] The brain makes adjustments to maintain its most stable state, and the body functions respond to the flow of information from all systems by altering the frequency output in the brain. For example, if the brain gets the information that the heart isn't pumping as it should, it will compensate by raising Beta and sending signals to stimulate the blood pressure to rise. Good brain-wave synchrony indicates a high level of good communication between the brain and the entire body.

Besides turning off worry, another benefit of achieving brain wave synchrony is that it tends to slow the aging process by stimulating blood flow. James Hardt, a psychologist and researcher, suggests that hemispheric synchronization delays the aging process.[6] When the hemispheres are balanced, you feel no stress, which improves sleep. British researchers Graham and Elena Ewing have found that the more dominant Delta and Theta frequencies at night are involved in physiological regeneration and the maintenance of health. James Hardt of the Biocybernaut Institute in B.C. discovered that the Alpha frequency is important in slowing aging, and as this frequency begins to disappear, it announces impending death.[7] When the optimal brain state is achieved, peak performance in work, athletics, and performing arts is reached.

Finally, and most important to people plagued with anxiety, synchrony training for the whole brain state normalizes the nervous system so you can easily zoom in on important matters and zoom out at will instead of living in chronic hypervigilance or emergency mode. Your flexible attention allows you to avoid a stuck state of mind. Getting yourself into an optimal brain state is like waking up to the best of yourself. Worry stays away, you live in a state of flow, and everyday life is easier. Achieving the whole brain state leads to a deeper understanding, stability of perceptions, and mastery of your self. It builds your ability to recover from and inoculates you against life stressors. It's a state where you can easily access information and achieve great insight. You understand your needs, vulnerabilities, yearning, and desires, but they do not control you. In the whole brain state there is no room for worry or rumination or any other negative emotion. It is a state of mind that is more flexible in thinking and clearer than other ordinary states. In fact, the secret to living a worry-free life is practicing the whole brain state.

How do you get synchrony, specifically Alpha synchrony? You focus on what's not there instead of what is.

Get Instant Alpha

As we saw earlier, Les Fehmi discovered that when students focused on the space in a room, or the space between their fingers, or the space around their body, or the space in a picture frame, rather than the picture, the object-less attention caused a balanced blood flow in the students' brain and produced phase synchronous Alpha.[8] Focusing on empty space increases Alpha waves because when you focus on nothing, your brain cannot develop a story. When there is no story, there is no judgment, no worry, no anxiety, and no depression. Just soothing happiness.

There are three "empty-space" meditation exercises you can use to increase your synchronous Alpha. To avoid getting bored, use one exercise after another over three days and start again. Or you can select the one you like the best to repeat.

Exercise 1

1. Close your eyes and focus on the space within an empty cup for one minute.
2. Picture the word *white*, and then the word *black* floating in front of you on a mental screen. Focus on the space between these two words.
3. Focus on the space between your eyebrows for one minute.
4. Focus on the imaginary space in your head between your ears.

Now try to maintain a worry thought. Can you do it? Probably not. Just rest your attention in the space. It's actually almost impossible to have any thought at all when you're focusing on space.

Try this series of four steps for 3 to 5 minutes each day. Even spending just a short time focusing daily on empty space leads to a whole brain state. The entire time you're in this whole brain state, it will be impossible for you to worry. In time, the exercise should condition you to shut off the worry at will just by staring at space. Over the first week, notice how much better you feel. Keep using the exercises after that. You are reconditioning your brain to calm the nervous system enough so you can begin to enter higher states of awareness that may include better control over your breathing, body tension, and a complete lack of worry.

Exercise 2

Should you find yourself narrowly focusing on a problem, pull your attention back, visualize the problem, and imagine it floating in front of you. Notice the space around the problem. Now, expand your focus and watch the image get much smaller and the great space around it grow bigger. Focus only on the space now and imagine you are the space with all of the stars and planets. You will notice how you are so much more than any problem floating in space. You are the space that is everywhere.

Exercise 3

The best time to do this training is first thing in the morning and once in the afternoon before eating. It begins with you sitting comfortably in a chair and reading the following script.

Place your feet flat on the floor and get comfortable. Breathe easily and, with each exhalation, allow your comfort to deepen. Begin to notice the comfortable feeling developing in your head and body. Focus on the space between your eyes and the imaginary space inside your head between your ears. Move down the neck and imagine the space in your throat and now into your chest and around the heart. Feel the energy of your heart beating into the space out in front of you. Imagine the space between your fingers on your right hand and now on your left hand. Move your attention to your back and the imaginary space within around your spine all the way down to the buttocks.

Now, move your attention to the developing comfort in the stomach and imagine the space in and around your stomach. As your relaxation continues, move into the space in your pelvis and inside your legs all the way down to your feet. Imagine the space between your toes on the right foot. Now imagine the space between your toes on the left foot.

Now move your attention away from your body to the space around your body. Focus your attention on the space in the room between the walls. Move your attention to the space above your house. Imagine that you focus on the space between the earth and moon. And now between the moon and Mars. Take your attention to the space in our entire galaxy. Stay with this focus for a few moments.

Now, begin slowly to return all the way back from the galaxy to the space between the moon and Mars. Return to the space between the earth and the moon and back to the space above and around your house. Return your attention to the space within the room you are sitting and the space around your body.

Begin now to reconnect with your body and notice your back on the chair and your feet on the floor. When you are ready, come all the way back into the present time and place. Take your time to re-orient.[9]

Feel free to develop your own meditation script that gets you to focus on space. You'll see the best results if you practice twice per day for several weeks. Your stress levels should disappear quite quickly. With continued practice, you'll start to deepen your intuition, improve your relationships, stimulate physical healing, and perform at your peak every day.[10]

Shake It Off

When we experience intense stress, fear, or anger, our muscles tend to contract; our nervous system moves into high gear with the release of norepinephrine, cortisol, and adrenaline; and our body becomes rigid and taught. If you have pent-up tension in your body, you might experience mild muscle movements, shaking, tingling, sweating, emotions, or sudden anxious thoughts while you do these exercises. This is normal. When we begin to calm down, we often tremble or shake because we're releasing tension or suppressed feelings. Just allow them to come and know that the body is resetting itself and releasing tension you may have carried for a long while. If it happens frequently or bothers you, stop the session and come back to it later. Most people have only mild responses to open focus or none at all.

Allowing the body to shake naturally is important because severe stress shuts down the Broca's area in the brain, which is the part that determines your ability to speak. If you're trying to express your feelings about a stressful event but you can't, it will just make you feel worse. Wait until you calm down and the shaking is over before trying to share your feelings first to yourself and then to a friend. If you don't allow your body to finish shaking, deep fears could remain in your unconscious mind, and they may be expressed in unsettled feelings. Clearing tension and stress leaves you more flexible and less reactive, which helps you develop more resilience and claim your birthright of feeling worthwhile and deserving to live life in happiness and joy.

As you learn how to control your mind, you will have more power and resilience in everyday life.

Resilience

Practicing the whole brain state has many benefits, one of which is resilience. Resilience is the ability to bounce back from an upsetting event, which includes resetting the nervous system without being left with enormous worry. Practicing the whole brain state gives the brain more flexibility in shifting mental states, which makes us more resilient to everyday stressors.

Although this next suggestion sounds outlandish, once you've stopped shaking from a stressful event, play a game of Tetris or some video game that completely absorbs your attention. The games inoculate against the tendency to compulsively review the stress of what happened. By engaging your visual system in a game that takes a lot of attention to play, it interferes with the brain's tendency to review negative events.[11]

Whole Brain State and Your Potential

If you're a worrier, unless you train your mind, a stressful event is bound to cause a reactive looping of worry thoughts that keep you locked into suffering. Practicing the whole brain state re-conditions how you react to emotional stress. When you can keep your arousal low in the face of upsetting events or stressors, your brain will store the memory in a nice, neutral box at the back of your mental closet. Without that intense charge attached to it, it can't come roaring back to trigger worry the next time you face a negative experience. The fewer negatively charged memories you experience, the less you'll overreact and the calmer you will be as you walk through life. In a state of lowered arousal, stored charged memories are processed and placed into the past without the charge associated with them. More of your attention is then available for other endeavors. When the whole brain functions in concert, you develop more psychological stability and emotional maturity.

How It Works in the Real World

Focusing on space works quickly, but it must be practiced to see long-lasting results. Learning to quickly shift your attention allows you to move in and out of a resting state and heal stress-caused problems. When you open or narrow your focus of attention, you manage potentially overwhelming stimuli each day. The more neuro-synchrony you have, the happier you are and the more you raise your awareness of novel responses to situations. Brain synchrony also allows you to use innovative thinking to solve challenges. When you are in the whole brain state in synchronous Alpha and don't know what to do, you feel confident that you can devise a solution for the most difficult problems. Because the whole brain leads to optimal functioning, you move beyond conditioned responses, and can see the big picture with greater clarity, organization, and intuition. Then you actually practice a new self.

Whole brain synchrony—and the perspective and problem-solving it helps us achieve—may have saved one of our client's lives. Jean was overwhelmed with worry when she came to see us. She was married to an emotionally abusive man. Among other things, he'd play mental games where he'd berate her, and then deny the behavior when she confronted him about it. On occasion, she'd come home and notice items she had put in specific places, like pictures hung in particular rooms, had been moved to different locations in the house. All of these surreptitious but not completely provable experiences led Jean to live in constant worry and fear. Because her husband had worked for a private investigator, he knew how to tap phone lines and perform undercover operations to gather information. Jean was sure he tapped her phone line. After years of this kind of gas lighting, she began to believe that something was wrong with her mind. Finally she worked up the strength to leave him.

She couldn't sleep well, and was fatigued from constant fretful worry. After practicing the first few tools in this book for four weeks, Jean was able to calm her mind enough so she began to sleep better, and she found the strength to start saving herself. She moved into in a gated community where her husband couldn't get to her. There she met a new man who ran a security company. He taught Jean protective measures to keep from her husband from intruding on her privacy. As she worked with us and discovered her mind was strong and her perceptions were clear, she started trusting herself more, gained a sense of empowerment, and devised a plan so she could live a happier life. Ultimately she divorced her husband and claimed a new life for herself, which included a wonderful relationship with the man who helped her. While we began with the early exercises in calming her anxiety, she moved from being frozen with terror and worry to taking action and saving herself by practicing the whole brain state. Some time after this mental training, Jean's ex-husband called her to ask for information about their daughter. In the past, she would have frozen in terror. This time she told him that he would need to call their daughter, and she held her boundary when he became verbally abusive and hung up on him.

Physiology impacts your psychology, so as you increase Alpha synchrony, other positive changes show up. You become open to your feelings, connect to your strength and your truth, and you are unafraid to know yourself. You see possibilities and a positive future. You feel balanced and at peace with yourself and your environment, and you bounce back from challenges and design good solutions.

Regulate the State and Content of Your Thoughts

Your goal should always be to train your attention in order to regulate both your mental state and your particular thoughts. As we have discussed, your internal state is reflected in the brainwave pattern, and thoughts are constructed from emotions, perspectives, and attitudes. Shifting the Beta content (often worry) by calming the mind and moving into Alpha and Theta states where images, daydreams, or feelings and more awareness occur regularly opens the gateway to unconscious wisdom and creativity. As you move more into Alpha over time, you can add Beta back by thinking about your experience or images, but your Beta mind is much more settled.

Alpha synchrony is associated with clear thinking. Technology and infrastructure have given us the hardware to experience harmonious relationships and live for longer periods in bliss and peace. What we need to learn now is the right software of thinking and our mental states. When partners share Alpha synchrony, they are less self-critical and more tolerant of their partner's weaknesses. In our clinic, when we hooked up couples to the same biofeedback system, and they both created synchronous Alpha, they reported feeling as close to each other as they did when they first got together. By sharing any of the exercises with your partner, both of you can enter similar states and over time, experience stronger bonds and less edginess with each other.

Sharing in calm Alpha states among executive teams, parents, and children, or others trying to work out conflict tends to facilitate cooperation. When two people experience Alpha together, all notion of threat from each other dissolves and clear thinking replaces worry and fear.

Practicing the whole brain state and the discipline to achieve this state brings you to a place of maturity and real mental fitness. The whole brain state enables you to resolve past hurts and yearnings, shore up any feelings of inadequacy, keep worry at bay, and achieve great levels of awareness. But once you can move into states of self-transcendence and maintain deep states of mind for increasing periods of time, you'll be able to eliminate chaotic thought, avoid emotional drama, and access wisdom, clarity, resilience, and bliss. The result is a self-regulated and happier life.

After practice, focusing on space, allow yourself to get lost in a pleasurable activity. Allowing yourself to become absorbed in an activity, whether music, work, or exercise, extends the amount of time you spend in the whole brain state. Often a shift occurs that opens you into a greater feeling of being alive, and life seems richer. You become aware of how everyone and everything is connected and in an expanded state of awareness; you realize that there is only this moment. You take control of your life by realizing you construct each day's perceptions, and you begin to perceive the world as one of many possibilities.

All around the world, researchers are investigating how higher states of consciousness and altered states of mind can get us closer to optimal states of performance. These are the states of long-term meditators, monks, and mystics who have what seem like superpowers. These optimal states create the super minds of athletes, performing artists, and entrepreneurs. They move into transformative states of consciousness and often have numinous experiences that in the present science-dogma are outside the paradigm of what seems possible. These higher states of mind take these advanced mind/body practitioners beyond linear time and into a state of unity where the self-boundaries disappear. Through a certain kind of focus and elevated state, the mind matures and wakes up to a greater reality. We begin to have a hint of these possible states for the ordinary person through the state of flow, which we discuss in Chapter 9.

Power Thought: *Focusing on empty space creates whole brain awareness–solutions.*

CHAPTER 9

Flow Into SuperMind

You can learn to turn on the flow state
to transform your daily life.
—Herbert Benson, *The Breakout Principle*

Johanna was an outstanding violinist. She had played the instrument since she was a small child. Because she loved to play, she practiced for hours, but over time she started feeling pain in her hand and wrist. Her teachers told her she was trying too hard and that the stress was affecting the way she held her bow, causing cramps and carpal tunnel syndrome. But Johanna knew something her teachers did not. She wasn't stressed because she was trying too hard; she was stressed because her bow hand had started to shake from an inherited neurological condition that caused tremors, and it was taking all her effort to control it. Her worry about the tremors caused her to stress out even more, which threw additional tension into her hands. She started worrying so much about it, it affected her performance during competitions. Fearful of ruining her career before it had even really started, Johanna came to see Bill, who suggested that clinical hypnosis might help her cope.

Bill taught Johanna how to put herself into a trance when she picked up her instrument to play. When she would play the violin in this alert but relaxed and focused state, the familial tremor would disappear and she would enter into a state of "flow," so absorbed in the music that she lost all track of time and her surroundings. The hypnotherapy allowed her to practice without tension, and as she became good at triggering the trance on cue, she began to replicate the same relaxed state while playing professionally. In a trance, she could focus on what she enjoyed and what she could control rather than worry about what a judge or audience would think. She knew when she made mistakes, but she had the strength to move past them and not linger over her errors. Johanna became so good at putting herself into a trance that no one knew what she was doing except her mother and Bill. Only a trained clinician would have recognized the signs: the slight dilation of the pupils, the relaxed attentiveness, a lack of muscle stress, and extreme focus.

Later, Bill taught Johanna to rapidly shift her focus back and forth between the music and the audience to draw them in to her contagious expressiveness. Communicating with the audience in this personal way allowed her and her listeners to intimately share the experience and enter into a collective state of flow. She gained professional acclaim and played with some of the world's most famous musicians. Her career soared while she learned to control her own brain and eliminate the tremor while she played, though it did return as soon she was no longer in a trance state.

Johanna was not only able to recover her confidence, she also was able to recover her love for playing, the whole reason she became a violinist in the first place. You could say that flow gave her back her mojo. It can do the same for all of us.

In the previous chapter, we explored the concept of the whole brain state. Physician and neuroscientist Alan Watkins, the director of the Complete Coherence Institute in Britain, suggested that this state of coherence is the biological underpinning of what elite performers call "the flow state."[1] Flow, a term coined by Mikaly Csikszentmihalyi, author, professor, and former chair of the University of Chicago Department of Psychology, is the opposite of Mind Wandering. It is the word he used to describe the state we are in when we're so involved in an activity, when our attention is so hyper alert and narrowly focused, that time seems to disappear.[2] Others might call it the zone, the runner's high, or the martial arts' *mushin* (no mind). It's the state we're in when we're reading a really good book and don't realize that three hours have passed. We naturally move into flow states whenever a task is pleasurable and takes intense focus; it is a transcendent state where we are at one with an activity. In fact Martin Seligman, author of *Learned Optimism* and *Authentic Happiness,* called flow the maximum state of positive emotion.

There are nine characteristics of the flow state[3]:

1. You feel that you are performing at the perfect level of your abilities, where you're not coasting but not too challenged, either.
2. You've merged so much with your activity you can't judge yourself.
3. You have clear goals.
4. You receive body/mind feedback; that is, you're aware of your success and failure so you can make adjustments.
5. You have complete concentration and focus.
6. You experience a total sense of control.
7. You lose all self-consciousness.
8. Your perception of time is altered.
9. Your task is an autotelic experience; that is, the task has intrinsic enjoyment.

The flow state is now thought to exist on a continuum beginning with micro flow states, where you are absorbed in an activity and lose track of time, to more intense flow states, where you have such difficulty separating yourself from an activity that your sense of reality is altered. We can enter flow states many times a day, any time we go into a state of narrowed focus and become so absorbed in what we're doing there is no sense of passing time. However, flow is connected to our biological ultradian cycle, the 90- to 120-minute cycles through which our cognitive processes surge and fade. The struggle and flow phases of the cycle are periods of activity, and the release and recovery phases are breaks in the flow state. Our brains can focus intensely for around 50 minutes, but then we enter a phase-down period where we automatically move into a state of absorption or trance. In this phase we often stare into space. Then our mind wanders, and sleepiness and mental "fuzzies" take over. At that moment we need to take at least a 20-minute break, where we completely change channels and concentrate on something new, or rest or take a walk. When we try to push ourselves beyond our recovery state, we stress ourselves and make it hard to retrieve flow again later.

Why It's Good to Go With the Flow

Recently in Scotland we experimented with accessing flow by doing the Bungee Bounce. A chest and thigh harness that were connected to rubber tubes and hooked 50 feet up to a geodesic dome structure strapped us in safely. We began to fling ourselves high up in the air and bounce on the rubber mat on the ground to fly higher on the upswing. The experience was exhilarating and lasted only three minutes, but we lost track of time and blended with the activity. Afterward, the feeling was amazing. We felt high on our own brain chemicals. Try as we might, it was impossible to conjure up a worry, angry, or fearful thought. The energized feeling and moving beyond the physical limitations of gravity left us emotionally lighter. We were left feeling completely confident and worry-free for an hour and a half. As the feeling faded, it became a resourceful memory to draw upon in the future. This activity is similar to the many movements in the flow genome project where the leaders work with people standing on exercise balls, and in devices used to turn them upside down.[4] The time it takes to create the flow state can be relatively short.

Dr. Csikszentmihalyi researched people for whom achieving flow is key to their success and renown—athletes, artists, dancers, gamers, rock climbers, and others—and discovered that those who enjoyed the most peak experiences, or flow, were also the most worry-free. They were unafraid to pursue challenging experiences and felt little fear of the unknown. In fact, he learned that our sense of flow, as well as its duration, tends to intensify as the physical activity in which we engage becomes more challenging and contains some added danger. They also had a high sense of fulfillment and were good problem-solvers.[5]

His flow research found that for an activity to trigger flow, it must make us stretch a bit to reach our goals but not be too hard that it raises our anxiety. Conversely, if the challenge is too easy, we risk becoming bored. Only when we are able to strike the right balance between a challenge and our skill can we enter into the ecstasy of flow.

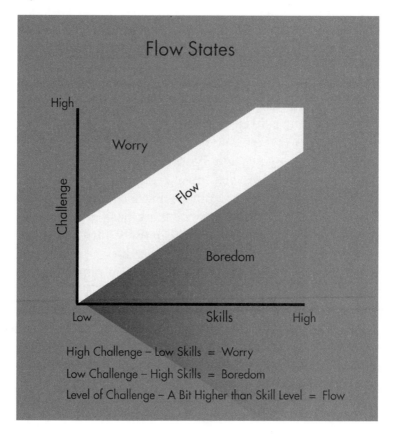

What does any of this have to do with our research on the effects of worry? Over the years, we, too have studied the cognitive state of athletes and peak performers at our clinic, and we confirmed something else Dr. Csikszentmihalyi discovered: It is impossible to conjure worry or any negative feelings, indecisive motivation, or intrusive thoughts when in a state of flow.

Not only have we found flow to be seminal to keeping worry at bay, we have found it sustains ideal performance and stimulates mental and physical healing. The more flow experiences you have, the more alive you feel. Since, as Czikszentmihalyi discovered, people who enjoy peak experiences often also suffer little from worry, we've concluded that an excellent way to banish worry is to try to incorporate flow into our everyday lives.

How does flow block worry? Quite simply, it's impossible to concentrate intensely on an enjoyable activity and worry at the same time. When you cross over from mere enjoyment to the flow state, you actually alter your awareness of the world around you. Things seem less frightening, and challenges less daunting, because flow cancels all the conditioned mental programs that limit your beliefs, moving you into a state where all possibilities and no dichotomies exist. In the flow process, the brain moves through all of the frequencies—Beta, Alpha, Theta, Delta, and Gamma—and your conscious mind shuts down judgment. Alpha waves calm the nervous system and Beta puts you in a state of alert relaxation like you might have if you were, say, playing tennis. Theta waves silence your inner critic, the "uh-ohs" or negative thought, and your worry. You even sense less pain because in this stage the brain releases natural painkillers. Your sense of self momentarily disappears; you and the activity have no separation. If you play baseball, you, the pitcher, and the ball are one. If you are a musician, you, the instrument, and the music are one. In addition, flow increases creativity. When you enter a state of flow, your mind begins to call up novel ideas and interesting ways of thinking about issues that open up new possibilities. Flow leads to heightened pattern recognition. In fact, a conductor who intentionally trains his choir to enter the flow state will often elicit better sound and flexibility of expression.

Flow is not just something experienced by performing artists, writers, and musicians, and religious leaders, though. One research study found that flow increased intrinsic motivation and self-determination with architecture and business students.[6] A 10-year study done by McKinsey found that business executives were five times more productive when in flow, and employees in flow make the best teams for a company.[7] Blending together and working as one entity helps team members lose their egos and shut off their worry and fear.

Intentionally working to trigger flow is important because flow experiences increase your willpower to break bad habits and accomplish extraordinary feats. Often when you are on the edge of a breakthrough to living in the next level, flow helps you stretch a bit farther to make it happen.

In flow, truly remarkable things are possible. For example, in his book *The Rise of Superman: Decoding the Science of Ultimate Performance,* Steven Kotler attributed some extreme sports achievements and personal life successes to flow, such as space diver Felix Baumgartner, who took a supersonic free fall in a special suit from the edge of space and survived. The experiment demonstrated a potential evacuation strategy for astronauts if their space ship failed. Less risky but effective is the use of neurofeedback by executives in business to develop more peak performance.[8] But you can achieve flow in simple ways such as exercise, meditation, or self-hypnosis. The extreme clarity and calm emotional detachment of flow increases performance, problem-solving, and creativity days after the flow activity. The reason is that while in flow we unconsciously make problem-solving adjustments in a nano-moment, but later, even when we're no longer in flow, we feel the aftereffects and continue to see alternative routes to our goals. And when we've consistently felt like we've made good decisions, our confidence and belief in ourselves goes up, and our worry goes down. So it's in our best interest to get to a state of flow as often as possible.

Unfortunately, flow can be lost if you are easily shaken by self-doubt or other people's judgment. The good news is, like every other mental state, we can train ourselves to enter a state of flow at will.

Overcoming the Mind's Limitations

Gary was a talented pole-vaulter attending college on an athletic scholarship. His brother, also a pole-vaulter, preceded him by four years and had set a high standard for achievement. Gary felt burdened by pressure from his brother's accomplishments. As a result, he couldn't jump beyond a certain height. His coach, felt certain Gary could do better, and referred him to Bill for hypnotherapy to help him overcome his mental block.

Bill discovered that in Gary's mental movies, he was constantly failing to exceed his own previous accomplishments. After putting Gary into a trance, Bill asked him to review his favorite vault. His eyes closed, Gary began smiling and using his hands to unconsciously hold an imaginary pole. To remind him what he was capable of, Bill asked Gary to mentally review other jumps he'd successfully made.

Finally Bill pointed out, "When you stand on the runway, you really don't know exactly how high the bar is even though you are told the height, and when you clear the bar, there is always room to spare." This suggestion helped Gary move his mind away from how high the bar was and focus on the automatic activity of running and planting the pole and vaulting. Just visualizing himself succeeding made Gary feel confident that he could accomplish the next vault goal. Bill suggested that he remember this feeling whenever he picked up the pole and felt it in his hands. He should remember how he felt in this state, thus creating a hypnotic trigger for the flow state the moment he feels the pole in his hands.

The next day, Gary's coach called Bill to tell him Gary cleared a height 6 inches higher than he ever had before. The day after that, the coach called to say that Gary had cleared an additional 6 inches of height.

Gary achieved peak performance by shifting his attitude, learning how to quickly clear his head of doubt and worry, and learning to enter into the flow state at will.

Cycle of Flow

Harvard psychiatrist Herbert Benson found that the brain activates different waves on the way to achieving the flow state, which he called "breakout."[9] In other words, to get to that low Alpha, high Theta brain state, you have to transition through many of the same brain-wave stages we've covered in this book. According to Benson, stage one of the cycle is the struggle phase. Everyone struggles when they're trying to solve a problem, have a better athletic performance, learn a piece of new music, or sit down to write a book. That struggle can frequently lead to worry. This stage triggers higher Beta frequency, causing stress hormones to flood into the system, such as epinephrine and norepinephrine. Our blood vessels constrict, and our heart rate and blood pressure go up. This is how the fight or flight reaction manifests itself when you are trying to solve a problem.

Stage two of the flow cycle is the release phase, in which you begin to let go of the stress and create more Alpha frequencies. In a process similar to the Mind Wandering we discussed in Chapter 3, you completely leave the problem you have been working on and focus your attention on something pleasurable, like taking a walk in the park, or anything calming that takes your attention away for a little while from the challenge at hand. In this stage, nitric oxide releases into the system and sweeps out the stress hormones.

Stage three stimulates the Theta and Gamma frequencies. Coinciding with these frequencies is the release of dopamine and anandamide, which as we discussed in Chapter 4 is in the family of endocannabinoids. They have been shown to help us heal, even if only via placebo effect, because we produce them when we *believe* we are taking or doing something that will make us feel better. In this stage, we also release endorphins that produce feelings of well-being. It is in this stage that we give up the struggle for control over our performance.

Finally, stage four is the recovery stage in which the brain stimulates the Delta frequency and releases serotonin and oxytocin. Serotonin is the neurotransmitter often associated with good mood, and oxytocin releases during bonding experiences. It is in stage four that you move into improved "new-normal" patterns. Flow changes old thoughts and emotional patterns, reduces your stress response, and releases enormous healing power in your body so you don't go back to your old worry self. In fact, you can't return to the old you.

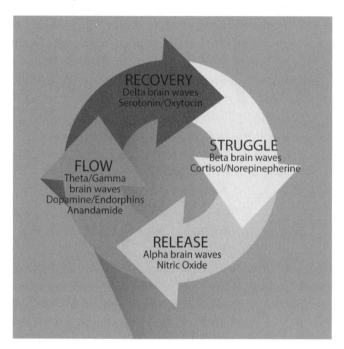

How to Start Triggering Flow

Remember: People who are stuck in a worry mind need to begin with the early exercises in this book so they can start by interrupting a pattern. Then they need to re-associate new possibilities to break out of their limitations, and re-pattern and condition themselves to reach positive states. Only then are you prepared to work on flow. You are building mental muscle so you can achieve the state of flow more regularly. The question is: How do we train this expanded state of awareness?

Depending on where you are in your own emotional mastery, many activities can trigger the beginning flow state, from jogging, visiting a cathedral, being in nature meditating or praying, or remembering a beautiful place you visited in the past. You could repeat a mantra or special word for a few minutes. You could lose yourself in a pleasant experience, including visiting a novel and tranquil place. You could volunteer. Focusing on a particular sound or visual image, especially a work of art or architecture, or listening to classical music, stimulates the initial flow state. Yoga, meditation, or martial arts practice opens flow states. Training in extreme sports, including running, skiing, or skydiving, can lead to intense flow states. Though less risky, singing in a choir or playing a kind of music where your focus demands that you blend into a group can give you an intense flow state. Even reading, solving puzzles, or playing computer games (Luminosity is a good website for this) can trigger flow.

It doesn't actually matter what you do, so long as it's a pleasurable activity that requires your undivided attention. As you get better at your activity, keep pushing your goals further so you continue to challenge yourself and you don't get bored. That said, don't set impossible standards, either. You always want to be practicing right in the sweet spot of your abilities, where you're challenged but not so frustrated you're tempted to give up.

Hypnosis

Several of Bill's worried clients have achieved peace and peak perfection by learning how to hypnotize themselves. Why did Bill suggest hypnosis? Because it takes you through similar brain stages as flow. When you are in a trance state, you cannot worry.

No doubt you have had the experience of watching a movie and losing track of time. Perhaps, you have been driving and lost in thought, momentarily forgetting where you are. These are hypnotic states of mind where consciousness is altered and your perceived reality shifts. Although researchers and experts in the field disagree about how to precisely define a trance, there is a general agreement that hypnosis entails:

1. A shift from broad focus to narrow or highly focused attention.
2. The use of memory and imagination.

3. A shift from conscious behavior to automatic. All hypnosis is self-hypnosis. Even when therapists place clients under hypnosis, they actually invite clients to place themselves into a trance, whether it is through a specific induction or focusing on a spot on the wall until the eyes tire, or listening to a story. We see elements of hypnotic trance and trance behavior with athletes, musicians, other performers, and businesspeople and scientists when they perform at a high level. They are selectively attuned to information they need to carry out their particular task. They block out extraneous stimuli, lose track of time, find what they do pleasurable, even though it may be physically and emotionally demanding, and report being in the flow state or the "zone." The trance state is very similar to the state of flow.

In fact, Lars-Eric Unestahl, sports psychologist, suggested that the state of hypnosis was similar to the state athletes enter when they are performing at their best, and designed a sport psychology concept around this called the Ideal Performance State. He noticed that these athletes only attended to relevant tasks, experienced time distortion, no pain, and effortless actions.[10] This zone of optimal performance often is acquired through intense focus and the use of visualizing the perfect performance. By mentally reviewing a former great performance in detail before a new routine, the sports athlete or performing artist moves into the optimal state to repeat the best experience.

Try It Now

Read the instructions all the way through before you do this exercise. You may even want to record it and play it back so you can close your eyes and enjoy the whole process.

Sit in a comfortable chair with your feet on the floor. Take a moment and fix your eyes on a spot on the wall. Keep focusing and notice how your breathing shifts into a more relaxed and comfortable rhythm. As you continue to focus on the spot, your peripheral vision will disappear. Now close your eyes. Remember the last time you were engaged in an activity where you felt you were in the zone and flowing. Maybe you were playing a game, singing with a group, or playing a sport. Remember the activity in detail. Imagine the feeling of being completely absorbed in the experience in present time so that you lose yourself; you and the experience are one. There is no access to problems or worry. You are completely immersed in the activity and in the moment. You feel in the flow of the experience, and it is uplifting. Now make the flow feeling stronger by imagining that it is. Linger in this memory of being in a flow state, with this experience, for as long as you like. As you imagine the flow state experience in real time, you feel you are actually there. The experience seems like a dream that feels real.

When you are ready, allow yourself to come back slowly. Take a few breaths and feel your feet on the floor, your back on the chair, and notice in a moment that you are all the way back in the present time. Relax a bit longer before you get up.

Flow Helps Solve Problems

The unconscious mind may be our most valuable asset. It is the ultimate solution generator and co-creator of million-dollar ideas, works of art and music, and spectacular architectural designs. The unconscious mind is the driver for flow states.

Elmer Green, well-respected biofeedback developer and researcher of higher states of mind, developed a process he called "interrogating the unconscious mind." While in a relaxed state of mind, he frequently asked his unconscious for answers to math problems. He often found that in this state, spontaneous imagery popped into his mind that helped him solve problems. For example, he received astounding information that helped him answer a math problem that had been unsolved by experts for 100 years, and published the findings in the journal *Science*. Green believed that asking the unconscious mind for information while in a state of flow gives us access to a kind of mental library that contains all of the knowledge and information in the universe.[11] Here's an interesting experiment: If you want to find a book in your personal library, sit in a chair among the books and ask your unconscious mind to show you where it is. Without putting pressure on yourself, relax and peruse your bookshelf. Often you will suddenly notice the book title.

Lee Zlotoff, producer and writer of the popular *MacGyver* television show in the 1980s, discovered that flow could help him when he needed to access his creativity to develop scripts quickly. MacGyver was a non-violent action hero and always solved problems with simple tools and a presence of humor and humility. After the series ended, the character's popularity soared and became a global meme for turning "what you have into what you need."[12] Zlotoff accidentally discovered a powerful tool when he took his mind away from a problem by relaxing while taking a walk or a shower, only focusing on the present moment. In essence, he took himself into the second stage of flow. Frequently, he shifted into a fleeting third stage, which was the flow state. Several hours later creative ideas would emerge that would help him write the next script. He learned that his unconscious mind would always come up with new ideas. Zlotoff received new ideas from the unconscious where much information is accessed. He demonstrated one more time how anyone from any profession or walk of life has access to the creative mind from being in a state of flow.

Take an Incubation Break

When you need a new idea or to re-work some creative project, it is useful to take a break from the work itself and completely change your environment. By getting into nature and listening to music or exercising, you alter your awareness. When you interrupt your worrying about a solution, you let go of your struggle and move into a trance state of narrowed focus, or flow. The unconscious mind is essentially an idea incubator, constantly processing information and formulating new solutions to the problems that occupy your conscious mind. Incubation breaks, however, allow the unconscious mind to super speed new ideas without the interference of worry or fear that you won't come up with something new. In fact, you never have to worry that your unconscious won't give you solutions. The key is to get out of your own way by taking the mind into a calm state by taking a shower or a walk in the park. When you use this approach, you avoid worry and the tendency to force things to happen. The mind will give you plenty of ideas to solve most problems.

Over the last 10 years, there have been many studies done on incubation to enhance problem-solving. The results across the board have shown that unconscious associative processing has a generative power to bring disparate ideas, past experiences, and connections together to form new ideas. People often approach problems with limited information or trial and error approaches, and these tactics block the ability to think outside the box. A time of intense study is required in your area of expertise followed by letting go of the outcome you hope for. When you discover that everything you ever learned or experienced is recorded at the unconscious level, you begin to appreciate your available reservoir of internal resources that will put ideas together you could never have come up with consciously. With practice, when you enter flow, and at the same time achieve the whole brain state, worry disappears.

Simple Process to Receive Guidance From Your Unconscious

You can solve any problem and keep the flow state activated by following this protocol.

Begin the incubation process by occupying the conscious mind on something else without thinking about the problem. Ask a question of your unconscious mind and write it down. This might entail asking for new ideas for a creative project or a book or for guidance regarding a decision.

Spend several hours or wait until the next day to see what pops into your mind.

Ask your unconscious mind to give you the information when the time is appropriate. You may notice that some news article catches your attention or you have a fascinating dream. The information comes in a variety of ways.

Peak Performance in the Flow State

Jeffrey Fannin and Joe Dispenza found their advanced workshop students had similar flow state experiences when they worked with them in open focus training. This is the practice of focusing on space in a meditative state, which we discussed in Chapter 8, that creates the whole-brain mental state.[13]

Christopher Bergland, science writer and extreme athlete who investigates the zone state in performance, identified a state of extreme flow that he calls "superfluidity," which he believes is the source of his real breakthroughs in ultimate performance.[14] This is a state that is episodic and harder to come by, but once you experience it, you will find endless energy and feel completely unified with the activity. This experience only shows up after much mental and physical training so you must develop skills to operate from a state of mastery. Bergland mused about whether we could plug into a universal source of energy available to all of us. He noted that his experience was like the description in *Ecstasy in Secular and Religious Experiences* by Marghanti Laski, who found that the triggers for this intense flow state were found in nature around water, trees, dusk, sunrise, and bad weather. Flow frequently occurs when we place ourselves in more natural environments.

The Institute of HeartMath in California, interested in brain and heart communication, researched and measured energy fields that extended from the heart and the brain of every human. They found that these two organs influence each other and apparently have electromagnetic, electrical, and perhaps some unidentified energy fields that flood every cell in the body.[15] The brain's energy is enormous, but the heart's magnetic energy field is 500 to 5,000 times bigger than the magnetic field of the brain. This means that not only are our own bodies bathed in interacting energy fields, but when we are around others, our fields are interacting. This means when you enter flow, you invite others around you to share the state. When you turn off worry by shifting into flow, your fields extend further from the body. Science is discovering that the state of flow may be a bridge to that higher connection and potentially activates advanced human abilities. It is the path toward mastery of your mind, body, and biology,

When you practice flow by doing any of the activities we discussed, you open yourself to a life of no regrets. In our clinical work we found that it is possible to create a new self, almost without worry. When you spend time focusing on developing the best version of your self, you have greater possibilities in a future you most want to experience. This is your personal peak performance: life.

Final Thoughts

This whole book has been dedicated to showing you that your mind holds the secret code to living a worry-free life. Because you take your mind with you no matter where you are, changing your outer circumstances rarely changes your state of mind. But learning how to achieve a healthier mental state is the key to mental and physical peace.

Life mastery is the ultimate goal that completely changes your experience in the world. By managing your physiology, by controlling attention, through shifting your breathing, or refocusing your attention, and practicing the brain change tools we've discussed ultimately dissolves inner tension and allows you to enter the whole brain state in coherence. When you are in balance and flow, you'll feel no fear or worry. You'll operate from an inner state of calm peacefulness, and transform yourself. You positively influence others, your business, and your spirit.

You can live your life not only free from worry, but also beyond the old uncomfortable and often debilitating states into a more creative, productive, and, with practice, ultimately a more satisfying reality. The process we have described in this book, based in the latest neuroscience, tells you exactly how to make this happen. By learning to interrupt worry states, use neuro-association to connect new understandings, practice neuro-repatterning to condition new states of mind, practice the whole brain state, and, finally, trigger flow, you create a new you.

Excited? Accept our invitation to live with a worry-free mind.

NOTES

Chapter 1

1. Church, *The Genie in Your Genes.*
2. Freeman et al., Amygdala Responsivity
3. Lamott, 1997
4. Csikszentmihalyi, *Flow.*
5. Roxanna Erickson-Klein, personal conversation, 2015.
6. Didion, *We Tell Ourselves Stories in Order to Live.*
7. Brinol et al., "Treating Thoughts as Material Objects..."

Chapter 2

1. Goodwin, "Alcohol and Recall."
2. Rossi, *Psychobiology of Mind-Body Healing.*
3. Wolf et al., "Managing Perceptions of Distress at Work."
4. Hartmann, *Walking Your Blues Away.*
5. John Grinder, personal communication, 2016.
6. Shapiro, *Eye Movement Desentization and Reprocessing.*
7. Cuddy, *Presence.*

Chapter 3

1. Roxanna Erickson-Klein, personal communication. April, 2016.
2. Mooneyham and Schooler, "Mind-Wandering."
3. Schooler et al., "Chapter One: The Middle Way."
4. Epley, *Mindwise.*

5. Tang et al., "Short Term Meditation Induces White Matter Changes..."
6. Gilbert and Killingsworth, "Wandering Mind Not A Happy Mind."
7. Giblin et al., "Unexpected Benefits of Deciding by Mind Wandering."

Chapter 4

1. Crum et al., "Rethinking Stress."
2. Wisneski and Anderson, *The Scientific Basis of Integrative Medicine.*
3. Kotler, "Flow States and Creativity."
4. Peniston and Kulkosky, "Alpha-theta Brainwave Training."
5. Yerkes and Dodson, "The relation of strength of stimulus to rapidity of habit-formation."

Chapter 5

1. Huther, *The Compassionate Brain.*
2. Brogan, *A Mind of Your Own.*
3. Whitaker, *Anatomy of an Epidemic.*
4. Kirsch, The Emperor's New Drugs.
5. Canfield and Hansen, *Chicken Soup for the Soul.*

Chapter 6

1. Heller and LaPierre, *Healing Developmental Trauma.*
2. Panksepp, *Affective Neuroscience.*
3. Atkinson, *Emotional Intelligence in Couples Therapy.*
4. Schore, *Affect Regulation and the Repair of the Self.*

Chapter 7

1. Elliott, *The New Science of the Breath."*
2. McCraty et al., "The Coherent Heart."
3. Benson and Klipper, *The Relaxation Response.*
4. Sánchez-Villega et al., "The Effect of the Mediterranean Diet on Plasma Brain-Derived Neurotrophic Factor (BDNF) Levels."
5. Ho, *The Rainbow and the Worm.*
6. J.K. Rowling, Borders Online interview, *https://legacy.hp-lexicon.org/about/books/books-hp.html*
7. Davidson and Begley. *The Emotional Life of Your Brain.*
8. Louveau et al., "Structural and Functional Features of Central Nervous System Lymphatic States."
9. Bhasin et al., "Relaxation Response."
10. Peeke, *The Hunger Fix.*

11. Campbell and Osbon, *Reflections on the Art of Living.*
12. Green and Green, *Beyond Biofeedback and Self-Control.*
13. From the film *Finding Joe* by Patrick Takaya Solomon. Released by Balcony Releasing, Amherst, MA, 2011.

Chapter 8

1. Budzynski, Budzynski, Evans, and Abarbanel, *Introduction to Quantitative EEG and Neurofeedback.*
2. Wise, *Awakening the Mind.*
3. Fehmi and Robbins, *The Open-Focus Brain.*
4. Fannin and Williams, "Leading-Edge Neuroscience..."
5. Ewing et al., *Virtual Scanning.*
6. Hardt, *The Art of Smart Thinking.*
7. Ibid.
8. Fehmi and Robbins, *The Open-Focus Brain.*
9. Ibid.
10. Ibid.
11. Holmes et al., "Can Playing the Computer Game 'Tetris' Reduce the Build-Up of Flashbacks for Trauma?"

Chapter 9

1. Alan Watkins, *The Secret Science of Brilliant Leadership.*
2. Csikszentmihalyi," Flow: The Psychology of Optimal Experience"
3. Nakamura and Csikszentmihályi, "Flow Theory and Research."
4. Flow Genome Project, *www.flowgenome.com.*
5. Maggie Yi Guo, "Capturing Flow in the Business Classroom."
6. Cranston and Keller, "Increasing the Meaning Quotient of Work."
7. Kershaw and Wade, "Neurocoaching."
8. Kotler, "Flow States and Creativity."
9. Benson and Proctor, *The Breakout Principle.*
10. Unestahl, *Integrated Mental Training.*
11. Green and Green, *Biofeedback and States of Consciousness.*
12. Zlotoff, The MacGyver Method, *www.macbyvermethod.com.*
13. Dispenza, *You Are the Placebo.*
14. Bergland, "Superfluidity."
15. McCraty et.al, "The Coherent Heart."

BIBLIOGRAPHY

Arnsten, Amy F.T. "Stress Signaling Pathways That Impair Prefrontal Cortex Structure and Function." *Nature Reviews Neuroscience Nat Rev Neurosci* 10, No. 6 (2009): 410–22.

Atkinson, Brent. *Emotional Intelligence in Couples Therapy: Neurobiology and the Science of Intimate Relationships.* New York: W.W. Norton, 2005.

Baird, B., J. Smallwood, MD. Mrazek, Y. Kam, M. S. Franklin, and J.W. Schooler. "Inspired by Distraction: Mind Wandering Facilitates Creative Incubation." *Psychological Science* 23, No. 10 (2012): doi:10.1177/0956797612446024.

Bandler, Richard, and John Grinder. *The Structure of Magic.* Palo Alto, Calif.: Science and Behavior Books, 2005.

Benson, Herbert and Miriam Klipper. *The Relaxation Response.* New York: Harper Collins. 2009.

Benson, Herbert and William Proctor. *The Breakout Principle.* New York: Scribner, 2003.

Bergland, Christopher. "Superfluidity: The Psychology of Peak Performance." The Atheletes Way. *Psychology Today. www.psychologytoday.com/blog/the-athletes-way/201303/superfluidity-the-psychology-peak-performance.* 2013.

Bergland, Christopher. "The Psychology of Peak Performance." *Psychology Today*, March 20, 2013.

———. "Superfluidity: The Science and Psychology of Optimizing Flow." *Psychology Today*, July 1, 2016.

Bhasin, Manoj, Jeffrey Dusek, Chang Bei-Hung, Marie Joseph, John Denninger, Gregory Frichionne, Herbert Benson and Towia Libermann. "Relaxation Response Reduces Temporal

Transcriptome Changes in Energy Metabolism, Insulin Secretion and Inflammatory Passages." *Plos One.* (2013). *http://dx.doi.org /10.1371/journal.pone.0062817.*

Brinol, Pablo, Margarita Gasco, Richard Petty, and Javier Horcajo. "Treating Thoughts and Material Objects can Increase or Decrease Their Impact on Evaluation. *Psychological Science.* Vol. 24, No. 1 (2013): 41–47. doi: 10.1177/0956797612449176.

Brogan, Kelly, and Kristin Loberg. *A Mind of Your Own: The Truth about Depression and How Women Can Heal Their Bodies to Reclaim Their Lives.* New York: Harper Wave, 2016.

Budzynski, Thomas, Helen Kogan Budzynski, James R. Evans, and Andrew Abarbanel. *Introduction to Quantitative EEG and Neurofeedback: Advanced Theory and Applications.* Second Edition. Atlanta: Elsevier, 2008.

Burkett, Virginia, John Cummins, Robert Dickson, and Malcombe Skolnick. "An Open Clinical Operant Conditioning as an Adjunctive Therapy in the Treatment of Crack Cocaine Dependence." *Journal of Neurotherapy* 9, No. 2 (2005): 27–47.

Campbell, Joseph. (author) and Diane Osbon, (Ed.). *Reflections on the Art of Living: A Joseph Campbell Companion.* New York: Harper Perennial. 1995.

Canfield, Jack, and Hansen, Mark. *Chicken Soup for the Soul: Twentieth Anniversary Edition.* Santa Barbara, Ca. Chicken Soup for the Soul Publisher. 2012.

Church, Dawson. *The Genie in Your Genes: Epigenetic Medicine and the New Biology of Intention.* Santa Rosa, Calif.: Elite Books, 2007.

Collins, Allan M., and Elizabeth F. Loftus. "A Spreading-activation Theory of Semantic Processing." *Psychological Review* 82, No. 6 (1975): 407–25.

Cranston, Susie and Scott Keller. "Increasing the Meaning Quotient of Work." *Mckensie Quarterly*, January, 2012.

Crum, Alia J., Peter Salovey, and Shawn Achor. "Rethinking Stress: The Role of Mindsets in Determining the Stress Response." *Journal of Personality and Social Psychology* 104, No. 4 (2013): 716-33. doi:10.1037/a0031201.

Csikszentmihalyi, Mihaly. *Flow: The Psychology of Optimal Experience.* New York: Harper & Row, 1990.

Cuddy, Amy. *Presence: Bringing Your Boldest Self to Your Biggest Challenges.* New York: Little, Brown and Company, 2015.

Davidson, Richard and Sharon Begley. *The Emotional Life of Your Brain: How Its Unique Patterns Affect the Way You Think, Feel, and Live—and How You Can Change Them.* New York: Plume Publishing, 2012.

Didion, Joan. *We Tell Ourselves Stories in Order to Live.* New York: Everyman's Library, 2006.

Dispenza, Joe. *You Are the Placebo: Making Your Mind Matter.* Carlsbad, Calif.: Hay House, 2015.

Dweck, Carol S. *Mindset: How we can learn to fulfill our potential.* New York: Random House, 2006.

Elliott, Stephen *The New Science of the Breath: Coherent Breathing for Autonomic Nervous System Balance for Health and Well-Being.* Allen, Texas: Coherence Publishing, 2005.

Epley, Nicoloas. *Mindwise: Why We Misunderstand What Others Think, Believe, Feel, and Want.* New York: Vintage, 2015.

Ewing, Graham, Elena Ewing, and Alex Hankey. "Virtual Scanning: A New Method of Health Assessment and Treatment: Part I. Assessment." *The Journal of Alternative and Complementary Medicine* 13, No. 2 (2007): 271–85.

Fannin, Jeffrey and Robert M. Williams. Leading-Edge Neuroscience Reveals Significant Correlations Between Beliefs, the Whole-Brain State, and Psychotherapy. *CQ: The CAPA Quarterly* (2012): 14–32.

Farland, David. *The Runelords: The Sum of All Men.* New York: TOR Fantasy, 1999.

Fehmi, Les, and Jim Robbins. *The Open-focus Brain: Harnessing the Power of Attention to Heal Mind and Body.* Boston: Trumpeter, 2007.

Ferriss, Timothy. *The 4-hour Workweek.* New York: Random House, 2009.

Freeman, J. B., R. M. Stolier, Z.A. Ingbretsen, and E.A. Hehman. "Amygdala Responsivity to High-Level Social Information from Unseen Faces." *Journal of Neuroscience* 34, No. 32 (2014): 10573-0581.

Gallwey, W. Timothy, and Edward S. Hanzelik. *The Inner Game of Stress: Outsmart Life's Challenges, Fulfill Your Potential, Enjoy Yourself.* New York: Random House, 2009.

Giblin, Colleen E., Carey K. Morewedge, and Michael I. Norton. "Unexpected Benefits of Deciding by Mind Wandering." *Frontiers in Psychology,* No. 4 (2013).

Gilbert, Daniel, and Matthew Killingsworth. "Wandering Mind Not a Happy Mind." *Harvard Gazette,* November 11 (2010).

Glaser, Jay L., Joel L. Brind, Joseph H. Vogelman, Michael J. Eisner, Michael C. Dillbeck, R. Keith Wallace, Deepak Chopra, and Norman Orentreich. "Elevated Serum Dehydroepiandrosterone Sulfate Levels in Practitioners of the Transcendental Meditation (TM) and TM-Sidhi Programs." *J Behav Med Journal of Behavioral Medicine* 10, no. 160 (1987).

Goodwin, D. W., B. Powell, D. Bremer, H. Hoine, and J. Stern. "Alcohol and Recall: State-Dependent Effects in Man." *Science* 163, No. 3873 (1969): 1358–360.

Green, Elmer and Alyce Green, *Beyond Biofeedback and Self-Control.* Santa Barbara, CA: Knoll Publishers, 1989.

———. "Biofeedback and States of Consciousness." *Handbook of States of Consciousness.* Benjamin Wolman and Montague Ullman, eds. New York: an Nostrand Reinhold Company, 1986. 553–589.

Grueber, C. E., S. Nakagawa, R. J. Laws, and I. G. Jamieson. "Multimodel Inference in Ecology and Evolution: Challenges and Solutions." *Journal of Evolutionary Biology.* doi:10.1111/j.1420-9101 (2011).

Guggisberg, Adrian G., Johannes Mathis, Armin Schnider, and Christian W. Hess. "Why Do We Yawn?" *Neuroscience & Biobehavioral Reviews* 34, No. 8 (2010): 1267–276.

Guo, Yi Maggie, and Young K. Ro. "Capturing Flow in the Business Classroom." *Decision Sciences Journal of Innovative Education* 6, No. 2 (2008): 437–62.

Hardt, James. *The Art of Smart Thinking.* Santa Clara, Calif.: Biocybernaut Press. 2007.

Hartmann, Thom. *Walking Your Blues Away: How to Heal the Mind and Create Emotional Well-being.* Rochester, Vt.: Park Street Press, 2010.

Heller, Laurence and Aline LaPierre. *Healing Developmental Trauma: How Early Trauma Affects Self-Regulation, Self-Image, and the Capacity for Relationship.* Berkeley, Calif.: North Atlantic Books, 2012.

Ho, Mae-Wan, *The Rainbow and the Worm: The Physics of Organisms.* Hackensack, New Jersey: World Scientific Publishing Company, 2008.

Hobson, J. Allan. *The Dreaming Brain.* New York: Basic Books, 1989.

Holmes, Emily, Ella James, Thomas Coode-Bates, Catherine Deeprose. "Can Playing the Computer Game "Tetris" Reduce the Build-Up of Flashbacks for Trauma?" *Plos One.* January 7, 2009.

Huther, Gerald. *The Compassionate Brain: How Empathy Creates Intelligence.* Westville, South Africa. Trumpeter Books.

Kaufman, Scott B., and Jerome L. Singer. "Applying The Theory Of Successful Intelligence To Psychotherapy Training And Practice." *Imagination, Cognition and Personality* 23, No. 4 (2003): 325–55.

Kee, Ying Hwa, and C.k. John Wang. "Relationships between Mindfulness, Flow Dispositions and Mental Skills Adoption: A Cluster Analytic Approach." *Psychology of Sport and Exercise* 9, No. 4 (2008): 393–411.

Kershaw, Carol J., and J. William. Wade. *Brain Change Therapy: Clinical Interventions for Self-transformation.* New York: W.W. Norton, 2011.

Kershaw, Carol J., and J. William. Wade. Neurocoaching: Leadership Coaching Using Neurofeedback. *Neuroleadership Journal,* (2012): 1–7.

Kirsch, Irving. *The Emperor's New Drugs: Exploding the Antidepressant Myth.* New York: Basic Books, 2010.

Kotler S. "Flow States and Creativity | Psychology Today." *Psychology Today.* 2014. *www.psychologytoday.com/flow-states-and-creativity.*

Kotler, Steven. *The Rise of Superman: Decoding the Science of Ultimate Human Performance.* Seattle: Amazon Publishing, 2014.

Kounios, John, and Mark Beeman. *The Eureka Factor: Aha Moments, Creative Insight, and the Brain.* New York, Random House, 2015.

Lamott, Anne, "Three Month Reprieve," In Theresa Borchard, (Ed). *I Love Being a Mom: Treasured Stories, Memories, and Milestones.* New York: Doubleday. (2004): 46.

Langer, Ellen J. *Counter Clockwise: Mindful Health and the Power of Possibility.* New York: Ballantine Books, 2009.

Laski, Marghanita. *Ecstasy in Secular and Religious Experiences.* Los Angeles: J.P. Tarcher, 1990.

Liu, Richard T., and Lauren B. Alloy. "Stress Generation in Depression: A Systematic Review of the Empirical Literature and Recommendations for Future Study." *Clinical Psychology Review* 30, No. 5 (2010): 582–93.

Louveau, Antoine, Igor Smirnov, Timothy Keyes, Jacob Eccles, Sherin Rouhani, J. David Peske, Noel Derecki, David Castle, James Mandell, Kevin. Lee, Tajie Harris and Jonathan Kipnis. "Structural and Functional Features of Central Nervous System Lymphatic Vessels Nature." Published online June 1 2015, doi:10.1038/nature14432.

McCraty, Rollin, Mike Atkinson, Dana Tomasino, and Raymond Trevor Bradley. "The Coherent Heart: Heart-Brain Interactions, Psychophysiological Coherence, and the Emergence of System-Wide Order." *Integral Review* 5, No. 2 (2009): 110–15.

Mooneyham, Benjamin and Jonathan Schooler. "Mind Wandering Minimizes Mind Numbing: Reducing Semantic-satiation Effects through Absorptive Lapses of Attention." *Psychonomic Bulletin Review* 23, No.4 (2016): 1273–1279.

Morewedge, Carey K., Colleen E. Giblin, and Michael North. "Spontaneous thoughts, self-insight, meaning, attribution, judgement, and decision-making." *Journal of Experimental Psychology* 143, No.4 (2014).

Nakamura, Jeanne and Mihaly Csikszentmihályi. "Flow Theory and Research." *Handbook of Positive Psychology* by C. R. Snyder, Erik Wright, and Shane J. Lopez. New York: Oxford University Press, 2001. 195–206.

Nolen-Hoeksema, Susan, Blair E. Wisco, and Sonja Lyubomirsky. "Rethinking Rumination." *Perspectives on Psychological Science* 3, No. 5 (2008): 400–24.

Odou, Natasha, and Jay Brinker. "Exploring the Relationship between Rumination, Self-compassion, and Mood." *Self and Identity* 13, No. 4 (2014): 449–59.

Panksepp, Jaak. *Affective Neuroscience: The Foundations of Human and Animal Emotions.* New York: Oxford University Press, 1999.

Pates, John. "Effects Of Hypnosis On Flow States And Golf Performance." *Perceptual and Motor Skills PMS* 91, No. 7 (2000): 1057–75.

Peeke, Pamela. *The Hunger Fix: The 3-Stage Detox and Recovery Plan for Overeating and Food Addiction.* New York: Rodale Books, 2013.

Peniston, Eugene and Kulkosky, Paul. "Alpha-theta Brainwave Training and Beta Endorphin Levels in Alcoholics." *Alcoholism: Clinical and Experimental Results,* 13, (1989): 271–279.

Persaud, Raj. *Staying Sane: How to Make Your Mind Work for You.* New York: Bantam, 2001.

Rossi, Ernest Lawrence., and David Nimmons. *The 20-minute Break: Reduce Stress, Maximize Performance, and Improve Health and Emotional Well-being Using the New Science of Ultradian Rhythms.* New York: J.P. Tarcher, 1991.

Rossi, Ernest L. *Psychology of Mind-body Healing: New Concepts of Therapeutic Hypnosis.* New York: W.W. Norton, 1989.

Sánchez-Villegas A., C. Galbete, M. Martinez-González, J. Martinez, C.Razquin, J. Salas-Salvadó, R. Estruch, P. Buil-Cosiales, A. Martí. "The Effect of the Mediterranean Diet on Plasma Brain-Derived Neurotrophic Factor (BDNF) Levels: the Predimed-Navarra randomized trial." *Nutritional Neuroscience.* Sep. 14, No. 5 (2011): 195-201.

Schlegel, A., P. J. Kohler, S.V. Fogelson, P. Alexander, D. Konuthula, and P.U. Tse. "Network Structure and Dynamics of the Mental Workspace." *Proceedings of the National Academy of Sciences* 110, No. 40 (2013): 16277–6282. doi:10.1073/pnas.1311149110.

Schwartz, Gary E., and William L. Simon. *The Energy Healing Experiments: Science Reveals Our Natural Power to Heal.* New York: Atria Books, 2007.

Schooler, Jonathan, Michael D. Mrazek, Michael S. Franklin, Benjamin Baird, Benjamin W. Mooneyham, Claire Zedelius, James M. Broadway. "Chapter One—The Middle Way: Finding the Balance between Mindfulness and Mind-Wandering." *Psychology of Learning and Motivation* ,60 (2014): 1–33.

Schore, Allan. *Affect Regulation and the Repair of the Self.* (Norton Series on Interpersonal Neurobiology). New York: W.W. Norton, 2003

Shapiro, Francine. *Eye Movement Desentization and Reprocessing.* New York: Guilford, 1995.

———. *Getting past Your Past: Take Control of Your Life with Self-help Techniques from EMDR Therapy.* Emmaus, Penn.: Rodale Books, 2013.

Seligman, Martin. *Flourish: A Visionary New Understanding of Happiness and Wellbeing.* New York: Atria Books, 2012: 12.

Sheldrake, Rupert. *Dogs That Know When Their Owners Are Coming Home: Fully Updated and Revised.* New York: Broadway Books, 2011.

Shore, A. *Affect Regulation and the Origin of the Self: The Neurobiology of Emotional Development.* New York: Routledge.

Stahl, Stephen M. *Stahl's Essential Psychopharmacology: Neuroscientific Basis and Practical Application.* New York: Cambridge University Press, 2000.

Tang, Yi Yuan, Quilin Lu, Ziuan Geng, Elliott Stein, Yihong Yang, and Michael Posner. "Short-term Meditation Induces White Matter Changes in the Anterior Cingulate." *Proceedings of the National Academy of Science of the United States of America* ,107, No. 35, (2015):15649–15652

Thompson S., and S. Richer. How Yawning and Cortisol Regulates the Attentional Network. *J Neurosci Rehabil* 2, No. 1 (2015): 1–9.

Travis, Fred, and Jonathan Shear. "Focused Attention, Open Monitoring and Automatic Self-transcending: Categories to Organize Meditations from Vedic, Buddhist and Chinese Traditions." *Consciousness and Cognition* 19, No. 4 (2010): 1110–118.

Unestahl. L. *Integrated Mental Training.* Sweden: VEJE International Publ., 1998.

Van Der Kolk Bessel. *The Body Keeps the Score: Brain, Mind, and Body in the Healing of Trauma.* London: Penguin, 2015.

Watkins, Alan. *The Secret Science of Brilliant Leadership.* London: Kogan Page, 2013.

Wise, Anna. *Awakening the Mind: A Guide to Mastering the Power of Your Brain Waves.* New York: Jeremy Tarcher, 2002.

Wisneski, Leonard A., and Lucy Anderson. *The Scientific Basis of Integrative Medicine.* New York: CRC Press, 2005.

Whitaker, Robert. *Anatomy of an Epidemic: Magic Bullets, Psychiatric Drugs, and the Astonishing Rise of Mental Illness in America.* New York: Crown Publishers, 2010.

Wolf, Elizabeth Baily, Jooa Julia Lee, Sunita Sah, and Alison Wood Brooks. "Managing Perceptions of Distress at Work: Reframing Emotion as Passion." *Organizational Behavior and Human Decision Processes* (forthcoming).

Yaden, David B., Jonathan Iwry, Kelley J. Slack, Johannes C. Eichstaedt, Yukun Zhao, George E. Vaillant, and Andrew B. Newberg. "The Overview Effect: Awe and Self-transcendent Experience in Space Flight." *Psychology of Consciousness: Theory, Research, and Practice* 3, No. 1 (2016): 1–11. doi:10.1037/cns0000086.

Yaggie, Matthew, Larry Stevens, Seth Miller, Angela Abbott, Chad Woodruff, Mike Getchis, Sean Stevens, Leslie Sherlin, Brandon Keller, and Suzanne Daiss. "Electroencephalography Coherence, Memory Vividness, and Emotional Valence Effects of Bilateral Eye Movements During Unpleasant Memory Recall and Subsequent Free Association: Implications for Eye Movement Desensitization and Reprocessing." *Journal of EMDR Practice and Research J EMDR Prac Res* 9, No. 2 (2015).

Yehuda, Rachel, and Linda M. Bierer. "Transgenerational Transmission of Cortisol and PTSD Risk." *Progress in Brain Research Stress Hormones and Post Traumatic Stress Disorder Basic Studies and Clinical Perspectives*, (2008): 121–135.

Yerkes, Robert and John Dodson. "The relation of strength of stimulus to rapidity of habit-formation." *Journal of Comparative Neurology and Psychology, 18:* 459–482, 1908.

Zlotoff, Lee. The Macgyver Method. *www.macgyvermethod.com.*

INDEX

ABOUT THE AUTHORS

Carol Kershaw and Bill Wade are licensed mental health clinicians who ran a private practice in Houston, Texas, for 35 years. They specialize in translating the latest findings in the fields of neuroscience and neurobiology into simple, practical tools that people can apply to everyday situations, from personal and relational success to business and leadership achievement. They have been married to each other for more than 30 years, and run workshops and retreats on dissolving worry, shifting personal reality to states of possibility, activating the healing response for illness and pain, and creating a dynamic flow in life. They have taught in the states and in Canada, Chile, Italy, Spain, and Mexico.

Carol Kershaw, EdD, is co-director of the Milton H. Erickson Institute of Houston. She is a member of the American Psychological Association, and an Approved Consultant for the American Society of Clinical Hypnosis. She is board certified with the status of Fellow in EEG Biofeedback and is the author of *The Couple's Hypnotic Dance* and co-author with Bill of *Brain Change Therapy: Clinical Interventions for Self Transformation.*

Bill Wade, PhD, is co-director of the Milton H. Erickson Institute of Houston, and is licensed as both a marriage and family therapist and professional counselor, holding supervisory status with both licenses. He is a Clinical Fellow with the American Association for Marriage and Family Therapy and is a member and Approved

Consultant with the American Society of Clinical Hypnosis. Dr. Wade is co-author with Carol of *Brain Change Therapy: Clinical Interventions for Self Transformation.* He is a long time student of meditation.

You can visit their website at *www.drscarolandbill.com.*